HOW TO

LIVE AN AMAZING LIFE

Patrick McNally PhD

First Published 2012
Revised Edition 2018

Published by Power Training Corporation Pty Limited
PO BOX 446, Wyong, NSW, 2259, Australia
www.patrick-mcnally.com

Copyright © 2012 Patrick McNally.

All rights reserved, including the right to reproduce this book, or portions thereof, in any form. No part of this text may be reproduced, transmitted, downloaded, decompiled, reverse engineered, or stored in or introduced into any information storage and retrieval system, in any form or by any means, whether electronic or mechanical without the express written permission of the author.

The scanning, uploading, and distribution of this book via the Internet or via any other means without the permission of the publisher is illegal and punishable by law. Please purchase only authorized electronic editions, and do not participate in or encourage electronic piracy of copyrighted materials. The publisher does not have any control over and does not assume any responsibility for author or third-party websites or their content.

National Library of Australia Cataloguing–in-Publication Data
Self Help, Wealth

McNally, Patrick
How To Live An Amazing Life

ISBN 978-0-9871989-0-7

Disclaimer

This publication is designed to provide general information regarding the subject matter covered. However, rules, regulations, laws, practices and the interpretation of same often change or vary from country to country, state to state and company to company. Because each situation is different, the reader is advised to consult with his or her own health professional or advisor regarding that individual's specific situation and needs. Some of the techniques included in this book may not be suitable for people who suffer from epilepsy. Please consult your doctor if in doubt.

Neither the author nor the publisher assume any responsibility for any errors or omissions, nor do they represent or warrant that the information, ideas, plans, actions, suggestions, and methods of operation contained herein is in all cases true, accurate, appropriate, or legal. It is the reader's responsibility to consult with his or her own advisor before putting any of the enclosed information, ideas, or practices into action. The author and the publisher specifically disclaim any liability resulting from the use or application of the information contained in this book, and the information is not intended to serve as professional advice related to individual situations.

This book is the work of the author's experience and opinion. Names, characters, places and incidents are either the product of the author's imagination or are used fictitiously. Any resemblance to actual persons, living or dead, or to actual events or locales is entirely coincidental.

About The Author

Patrick McNally PhD is a Doctor of Philosophy, has a PhD in Psychology, is a Clinical Hypnotherapist, and is a licensed NLP Practitioner and Change Clinician.

Patrick works with the general public, sports stars, celebrities, politicians and corporate organisations. He has private practices in Sydney, New York and London.

Patrick is a regular on radio and television, having a regular segment on morning television for many years.

Patrick is best known for his outrageous methods to help people any way he can. He is dedicated to making sure that everyone knows How To Live An Amazing Life.

Patrick says, 'Today, people's needs are different so I use everything and anything that will produce an improved change for my client.

When someone comes to me and says, "I suffer from depression" I ask them if they brought it with them, or is it in their handbag or wallet? Sometimes a client will add that their depression runs in the family, so I ask them how many legs their depression has, two or four. It's a nice way to say, "G'day, look out, you are about to become happy again. It won't hurt a bit, I promise".

To contact Patrick, visit his website at
www.patrick-mcnally.com

Dedication

I dedicate this book to my older brother Tom McNally who obviously I've known all my life. As we both move into the second half of our journey as brothers, I look back with fond memories and gratitude to have had such a wonderful brother to look out for me all this time. Like all brothers we often didn't agree on things, but through it all we found each other again in the family love we inherited from our wonderful Mum and Dad. Your courage, strength, sense of humour and love will be forever in my heart. This is for you dear brother, we all miss you dearly.

20-5-1949 – 08-11-2012

Contents

The Amazing 60 Second Challenge 10
What Is Your Dream Life? 14
Is Your Life Already Amazing? 20
What Stops You From Living An Amazing Life? .. 24
    Childhood 24
    Education 24
    Age 25
    Beliefs 25
    Do You Secretly Suffer From Shame, Fear And Guilt 33
    Drugs Are Killing Us 36
The Importance You Place On Things 42
    The Amazing Grandmother 49
Your Body Plays Tricks On You 51
What Are Your Needs? 58
    Certainty 58
    Uncertainty or Variety 58
    Significance 58
    Connection 59
    Growth 59
    Contribution 59
The Power Of Feeling Truly Grateful 61
    Turning A Perceived Loss Into A Transition 64
How Suggestible Are You? 68
The Law Of Attraction 75
    Step 1 - Split your day into segments. 78
    Step Two – Deliberate Creation 79
    Step Three – Law Of Allowing 82
My Awakening 84
Spirituality Or Intuition 89
Amazing Relationships 94
    Negative People 99
    Your Significant Other 100
How To Become An Amazing Parent 102

The Amazing Bank Technique 104
   Change What Doesn't Work 106
   An Out of Control Teenager 108
   Remember You're the Parent 117
   Amazing Love Of A Child 119
Wealth **124**
   A Blueprint For Building Wealth 127
   Money 133
   Can You Own Your Own Business? 140
   Bankruptcy 143
Celebrities **146**
   The Day I Met a Superstar 149
Tips To Make You Feel Amazing **155**
   Model Success 155
   Plan It 155
   Fire It Up 155
   Believe It 156
   Good Or Bad 156
   Take Some Action 156
   Major In The Big Stuff 156
   Enjoy The Ride 157
Naked In Front Of The Mirror **158**
Conclusion **162**

If your life isn't where you want it to be I'm about to show you why, then show you how to get there

AMAZING - a·maz·ing - causing great surprise or wonder, astonishing, startlingly impressive, astounding, wonderful, surprising

The Amazing 60 Second Challenge

Welcome to an Amazing Life. I have started this book with what has now become my signature technique. I call it *The Amazing 60 Second Challenge*. By the way at the end of this I have a video link for you so you can watch me talk you through it. So if you need more explanation about this amazing technique, go the free video at the bottom of this.

For years now I have used this powerful technique with my clients. As well as demonstrating this in my practice I have presented it on television shows, radio programs, in front of audiences, with celebrities and in media interviews. So this proven technique that you are about to do will truly change the way you feel right now. I want you to know that every time I deliver this technique to people it changes that persons' entire perspective of what is possible in their life. That's how profound this wonderful technique is. Before you read this book, please do this technique now.

Step 1

Think of anything that is bothering you, worrying you, or making you feel sad or fearful. This can be anything at all. The bigger the problem the more change you will experience so don't hold back ... pick the worst think you are going through now.

Step 2

As you keep thinking about it, let yourself detect where you feel it in your body. Now the body can provide you with sensations anywhere, so don't be surprised if your body gives you an unusual place. Some people have found their body gave them sensations in their chest, arms, stomach, throat, between their breasts (females), or at the top of their stomach (men store it here a lot). Just become aware of where it enters your body.

Step 3

Next, I want you to detect in which direction this feeling is moving. It has to move – feelings move all the time. I just want you to become aware of the direction. For example, I want you to think about being nervous. When a person is nervous, they normally say "I have butterflies in my tummy". What they are really saying is "My tummy feels like it is moving in circles". Get my point now.

Step 4

By now you should be thinking of it, feeling it and know the direction in which it is moving. Now I want you to look at what it is you are seeing in your mind's eye. Is it a still picture or a movie?

Go to **a)** if it's a picture

Go to **b)** if it's a movie

a) If it's a picture, place a black border around the edge and move it away from you in your mind's eye, shrinking it down to the size of a postcard. Then move it away from you again until it's the size of a postage stamp. Then when it is as small as you can make it, take a deep breath and blow it away until you can't see it anymore. At the very same time as you are doing this, I want you to place your hands on the area of your body where the feelings are. Then push the feelings in your body in the opposite direction. So, for example, if you discovered the feelings were in your lower stomach moving up, you would use your hands to move the feelings downward. As you blow the picture away you should also find you have moved the feeling from your body.

b) If you see a movie playing all you need to do is pick the worst part of the movie and freeze it, just like using the pause button on a remote control. Now you have a picture and can continue with the technique by following the instructions given in **a)**.

Step 5

Test the results of your work. Try to think again about what was worrying you or bothering you and see and feel for yourself how remarkably different the experience is now.

This powerful technique can be used for many things. Practice it over and over again. If you have loved ones that are unhappy use this to help them. Have them do the technique while you move the feelings with *your hands,* which I might add is even more powerful. Make this technique a life skill by incorporating it into your life. I have used it on everyone from the general public to the most famous of clients and it always produces amazing results.

What Is Your Dream Life?

Would you like an amazing life like Mother Teresa? Caring for the dying. Would your amazing life be like Donald Trump, billions of dollars and a leader in industry? Or would your amazing life be a rock star? Do you want to own and operate your own business? I read about a mother who's dream was to raise her children in a way that impacted the world, so she raised her children to be world leaders, her name was Rose Kennedy.

Here is the first dilemma for many people who visit me. How do they pick what life they want? In fact many people are not aware they even have a choice. So many people have described to me over the years that their current life *just sort of happened*. Which to me means they didn't plan and one of the main reasons they didn't plan was they succumbed and subordinated to other people, especially parents, friends and family members who told them what they should or shouldn't do. Mostly what they *couldn't* do. These are the people who help take away another persons dreams in the first place.

Many of my clients have told me they hadn't noticed where their time had gone. One day they were at school feeling happy and carefree and the next thing they were adults. One person mentioned that she remembers one minute she was a teenager that went out and partied, then without realising time had moved on and she had become a parent with a mortgage. In the blink of an eye her life had moved on at such a rate she didn't feel in control at all. She was full of regret.

One of the first things people struggle with is defining the world they would love to create. Just like a painter or a musician, the word *create* to me means, *start with a blank canvas, or a blank computer screen*. The important word here is start, not wait around and let your life be used up. Don't wait another day to have an amazing life. Don't let another hour go past (one you will never see again) until you agree to take action on your amazing life. So to answer the question, how do you know what you want, imagine this.

Back in 1879 Edison didn't know how to create a light bulb did he? That's why it took him so many attempts. History is littered with similar stories about how men and women created lives that were worthwhile and filled with purpose, because they just didn't know any better.

So here's the wonderful news, you have already begun your creation and now together we will craft new pathways and opportunities for you to show your hidden talent and live an amazing life. You already have genius and a wealth of experience deep within you, the only thing you haven't done yet is cashed it in and seen the results. I'll show you how to do that as you continue to read on.

Inside these pages I promise you this. You will have no excuses not to live an amazing life. I'm now your private, personal and business coach and together we will take on the world and love each minute. Keep going back over this book again and again. There is so much here for you to keep gaining a new perspective on your life.

I have included the techniques used in my private practice and with my corporate clients. I know the techniques work and help people go on to live amazing lives and operate successful companies and enjoy wonderful relationships.

I've got three decades of proof that what you are about to read and experience truly does provide people with amazing lives. So I have no doubts about the outcome at the end of this book. Use my techniques and you will truly live an amazing life.

However, just because I have proof, doesn't mean to say you may not have your own doubts. You see if you do have any doubts you need to pop them away, keep them out of your head until you finish reading. Beliefs that create doubts are not useful when you read a book like this one, you will lose too much insight if you have doubt.

Imagine if you created doubt about crossing a busy road, or needing to go to the toilet. You see I know you can create doubt about all sorts of things, it's just I don't want any doubt when you read this. Just begin reading and take in all the information as it comes at you and enjoy learning new things.

When you have read this book you will totally understand how to change the way you feel anytime you want, instantaneously every time. By changing the way you feel you will change your behaviour, which means you can spend more positive time on your life.

It's not rocket science by the way, this business of self-help. Self-help means you and I in partnership work together. So before we start just take a moment to note how many self-help books you have read in your life so far. Then note how many seminars, workshops, training programs and courses you have attended, then work out how much of all that information you have put into your everyday lifestyle.

I'd hazard a guess that like millions of other people you haven't been able to put many of the self help tips into your everyday life have you? It's okay by the way because you and I are about to go on a real life-changing journey together.

My point here is that if the statistics tell us that you won't use many of these tips then why would I bother to include them? Many authors in the self-help business cram in as many as possible in the hope that some information might stick. I won't be doing that.

I will give you the tools that produce amazing results. I won't just say you *should* do this or you *should* do that. I believe in giving people the *how to*. This amazing life you are about to unleash will transform your life and those you love most, so just do the exercises.

I've only included the techniques and strategies that I use every day of my life with other people that change their lives and business. This way I know that when you include them they will be very easy to incorporate into your current lifestyle.

How many people have you seen that are on a fitness regime and go to the gym for a while then before long they have given up? The reason they gave up was because it wasn't incorporated into their lifestyle as a habit. It didn't become a way of life for them. It didn't become high enough on their priorities. They didn't make it part of their life.

My techniques will become everyday habits just like cleaning your teeth. Just remember though, your parents taught you how to clean your teeth. They reminded you plenty of times to go and clean your teeth. At first you probably didn't do it correct or not at all. Then as you became used to doing it, you did it yourself. Just like you learned to clean your teeth, you will learn to use these techniques because I'm going to be here all the time reminding you and urging you on.

I'm also a Hypnotist and because you now know I am, you also know that while you are reading this text, your mind will tend to wander from time to time, just like most minds do. So because you know I'm a Hypnotist you know that I will include phrases in this book that will go straight past your tiny conscious mind (your 7% voice). Because you know this and because I know you want to improve your life and that of your loved ones I will indeed include such phrases for you. And I know you don't mind.

Have you ever noticed when you are in a small group of people and someone is talking and the rest of you are listening, how easy it is to just drift away on your own? Well that is just what I'd love you to do while you and I journey onwards in this text. You'll also notice that I'll get to a part of the book and ask you to stop reading and complete an exercise. There is a very powerful reason for doing so by the way and I'll share that with you as we journey though. I will share with you what works for others.

I'll give you my very best and I know with certainty that if you take on these amazing techniques and practice them until they become a skill and eventually a habit, my work will change your life.

So let's keep discovering more.

Is Your Life Already Amazing?

If you were sat in my office now I'd ask you this question because from the very beginning I want you to realise your life means the world to me. It doesn't matter if you are a Politician, Sports Star, Celebrity or a Hairdresser. I have to know if you already think you are living a truly amazing life.

I'm now going to make an assumption that because you are reading this, you at least want to learn more about *how to live an amazing life*. Otherwise you could sit on your lounge and watch the television instead. So perhaps your life isn't amazing enough.

I'm in a unique position in that I work with a wide range of clients throughout the world, so I learn how these people live an amazing life. I ask them how they do it and how they maintain it. I have also met many people who don't live an amazing life, people who for one reason or other just can't find a way to live an amazing life.

I'll be including both sets of behaviours that both sets of people use. You will learn the traits of the rich and famous as well as understanding how others have not made their life amazing. I'll explain how they did that and how you can avoid it.

So let's begin. The first thing I'll ask you to do is rate your life as it is today. Rate it out of ten. So ten being amazing and one meaning your life is a disaster. The only number you can't use is five because I don't want you to sit on the fence and be average now do I?

Be honest, this is based on you and your life as it is today, not what you want it to be. These are the areas I want you to rate out of ten:

Your career/work/business	Rating _____
Your spousal relationship (if you have one)	Rating _____
Your family (how well you get on with each other)	Rating _____
Your Physical Health (weight/eating habits etc)	Rating _____
Your Mental Health (anxiety, depression etc)	Rating _____
Your Wealth (do you have financial independence)	Rating _____
Your Spiritual Self (do you feel connected)	Rating _____

If you were sat in my office I'd already know that at least one part of your life would be between two and four. Remember I'm a Therapist, I don't get visitors whose lives are totally amazing. They come to me because their life isn't where it should be. Clients never say one and they attempt to lie to me and say six, but I give them a look and they soon tell me the truth.

The interesting thing about rating where you are in your life right now is that we both have a starting point. I now know what to give you in terms of information. There is nothing worse than reading information that you already know. So now here is your next question. What needs to happen in your life for your rating number to rise up to eight or a nine? The people who sit opposite me often can't answer that question. This book will enable you to answer this question and many more.

Now while you are contemplating that question let me shatter some myths for you. If you live in a part of the world that we call western civilization then you would have been sold this myth since you were born.

You were sold that success equals fame, fortune and riches and perhaps other related materialistic items. You, like millions of others have been fed year after year the images of success. You witness flashy cars, beautiful healthy bodies, big homes, massive wealth and believe that this is an amazing life. So it goes without saying that unless people have these items they believe (wrongly) they don't live an amazing life.

So when you grow up and realise you don't have any of that, you rate your life against that model of the world. You see by rating yourself you need to run a comparison on what it should be or could be. Otherwise your rating number would have been nine or ten, especially if you compared your life to the homeless who live on the street.

When I begin to help a person live an amazing life there is a structure to it. My job is to demonstrate to my client how easy it is to make their life amazing. By the way, the reason it is so easy is there are so many examples of people living amazing lives all over the world. So here is the first of many ways I will teach you how to live an amazing life. Everyone I have ever met who lives an amazing life feels grateful. Yes sounds odd I bet, but these people who live amazing lives are very grateful people deep down in their soul. Sure like everyone they become upset and angry sometimes but the trend throughout all my research with them is they are very grateful. If you feel very grateful for the chance to live your amazing life you will grab that chance with both hands and enjoy the journey. Let me show you first what stops people living an amazing life.

What Stops You From Living An Amazing Life

You may or may not know what is currently stopping you from living an amazing life. So to help you work that out here are some of the things people have told me that have stopped them, perhaps they may resonate with you.

Childhood

This excuse is very popular with people who spend their life blaming their parents, their siblings or anyone they can think of. Now remember these grown adults who have made adult decisions about their own life, turn to me and tell me it was their upbringing that stops them living amazing lives. Can you believe that excuse? Yes I do understand the influence parents have on us and I'll be covering that in more detail later, but to use parents as an excuse is itself the very thing that does stop them.

Education

This excuse is given as if it is someone else's responsibility that they didn't have an education. I must admit I might sometimes take this one personally as my education didn't really kick off at all until my adult years. As a young boy I had dyslexia, but nobody knew. I still have trouble in that area to this day, that's why it's a difficult process writing a book. To make matters more difficult I was a brilliant soccer player in my youth, so teachers took me out of class daily to go and demonstrate all my soccer skills.

My father was a champion Irish footballer so he gave me his gift. However by aged 13 I was teaching Physical Education lessons at my school and never went back to another lesson myself. I played soccer every minute of every day for years and my education was as poor as it could have been.

So you can understand how I sit in my chair listening to this excuse and want to jump over the desk at some people, slap them and wake them up. If someone like me could re-educate myself anyone can.

Age

This excuse is a very powerful one because when a person creates this belief it can be difficult to dismantle. Be aware that both males and females often use this but for different reasons, at different times and for different outcomes. It appears that when people reach a certain age society dictates what they can and can't do. Don't get conned into thinking you have to retire, you don't have to.

Beliefs

A belief can lead someone to commit murder, not let their sick child have a blood transfusion, worship statues, fly airplanes into buildings, verbally abuse their loved ones and make their own life pitiful and much more.

So when a belief is sold to another human it can grow, and once that belief is sold to millions of humans, it can lead a country to invade another country and kill other humans who have not agreed with the belief or who haven't been sold the same belief.

Beliefs drive humans to behave in extraordinary ways.
- Do you know what beliefs are driving you as a human being?
- Do you know what beliefs are limiting you as a person?
- Do you believe the sun will come up again (even though the clouds may hide it)?
- If you answered yes, are you sure?
- If you answered yes, I'm sure, then are you sure enough to have some doubt? (How's your head after these questions?)

So I take it that you have a strong belief that the sun will rise every day. In your mind's eye you will have a place for your belief of the sun. If you were to close your eyes and think about your sun belief, you would discover that your unconscious mind would provide you with a representation of that belief. It may be a colour, a shape or a sound in your mind. Whatever it gives you, it is your representation of that belief. Because that belief is so strong, it's easy for your mind to provide you with its representation.

Now, I want you to think of something that you're not sure about. It could be that you think you believe it, but maybe you don't. Now as you think about this unclear belief, you'll find that your unconscious will provide you again with a representation of this belief in your mind's eye. Take a moment, close your eyes and think about this doubt for a while. As you think about it, find out what is different about it compared to your belief in the sun.

This second belief is not as strong as your belief in the sun, so your second belief will always be different than the belief of the sun. Here's the fun and easy part. If you want to make that second, doubtful belief into a strong belief, all you need to do is change it to the same as the sun belief. This might mean you have to move it into the same place you have the representation of the sun belief. If your sun belief is top right hand corner and a blue colour with a dark border then move your second belief there and change it so it is the same as your sun belief.

When you do this in a moment remember to look carefully at any little differences between your belief of the sun and this doubt. It could be that the image has more. Does your sun belief have sound for example? Or does it move around? The little differences are very important when you compare and then copy, so look closely for them. Go ahead and do that now.

Were you able to change your doubt into a stronger feeling of belief? You know when you do these exercises on your own, your conscious mind wants to interrupt you with remarks or questions about it all. For now just keep going with the exercises, you take control. When you have discovered the differences between these two all you need to do now is move your doubt over to where your strong belief is and bingo, you have just created yourself a much stronger belief.

Can you imagine what you can make possible in your life if you create a belief that drives you? Can you picture yourself being able to believe that you can have happiness, wealth, a loving relationship? Imagine what your life would be like when you decide to believe that you will stop taking drugs forever.

Imagine the feelings that will surge through every cell of your body when you believe that you are already wealthy and preparing for even more wealth. You see, when you believe something, your mind doesn't know if that belief is real or not. For example people with phobias create false fear and then believe it. So they are constantly believing something that is not real and tricking their mind.

Creating beliefs the way I do allows you to quickly and easily position a belief in your mind that your conscious mind will not question. Ultimately this belief will grow even stronger within you as you take action with your new behaviour and when you move it into a place of importance to you. By programming your beliefs fast and using your visual, auditory, kinesthetic, olfactory and taste senses, you are using the very essence of what makes you who you are.

In summary, to change a belief you first need to:
- Identify what that belief is and what benefit it provides you. It may be a positive or negative benefit. There will always be something or some reason at the end
- Close your eyes and relax thinking about the belief until you can see it and feel it in your minds eye
- Once you have that belief, place it to the side and clear your mind
- Create your new belief in your mind and add to it as you build it. See what you want to see, feel what you want to feel, until you have a very powerful state of mind
- Move the new belief over the old belief five times really fast

So now that we have completed this technique, let's see how you go with this one.

I want you to now go back in time and recall a memory that you'd like to change the way it makes you feel. It may well be a memory that is not that pleasant, and you don't mind changing it. Don't choose a happy memory, I want you to have a memory that is not such a good one. It might be an event or situation that's happened and you just want to change the way you feel about it now. So at the moment, remember how you feel about it now, because in a few moments time you're not going to feel the same way.

Now as you think of your memory you might have a picture of someone, or an event, or it might just be a symbol in your mind's eye. It could be a colour, it could be anything that has popped into your mind. Put the book down, close your eyes and remember the event, then open your eyes and pick the book back up again and continue.

Remember this is a *how to* book, so don't just sit there, get into it now. If you were sat opposite me right now I'd be urging you to do this. You have the book, inside the book holds the *how to*. Enjoy this next exercise.

Now I want you to imagine your memory as an event, if there were people connected with your memory then include them, and then run your memory as a movie. Run your memory as a movie in your mind's eye so you can see the event again. Make sure you can see what you were doing, see other people, and make sure you see yourself in the movie. Put the book down and do it, once you've accomplished that, open your eyes and read on.

Now you are going to change this memory. We know what our outcome is. Our outcome is to change how we feel about the memory. You know what a fairground or carnival is and the ride called a Merry-Go-Round? Now this ride normally plays a traditional type of music, and it's that music I'm going to ask you to play in your mind in a moment.

So far we have taken a memory from the past, we're in the present, and now we're going to program it to how we're going to feel about it in the future. So from then on every time you think of this memory, you will feel different than you do now. In a moment I want you to run the movie backwards at fast speed, and I want you to add the music. The music is the Merry-Go-Round ride. Play that music at the same time as you run this movie backwards really fast. See yourself and the entire movie going backwards. Everything is going backwards. Close your eyes and do that now, then read on.

Now, this time I want you to see yourself looking really silly, stupid even. I want you to see the other people looking stupid, see them making idiots of themselves, even falling over. The events are going backwards. In this movie that you are going to run backwards people have big green ears and big red noses. In this reverse movie you're laughing and smiling at what you can see. Run it all backwards. Look how stupid you look, see how funny, look how dumb it all is. Do it at triple the speed, that means really fast. And when you've done it, open your eyes. Put the book down and do it now.

So what you have done is remembered a memory and made a choice to change the way you feel about it. Remember, as humans we use feelings to drive us in our life. Now in a moment I'm going to ask you to close your eyes and think about the memory again. This time when you think about it, I want you to feel what's different about it. There may be music playing now, and people are moving backwards, falling over, and looking silly. How do you feel about that particular memory now? Does it affect you the same way? What difference has it made to the way you feel? Does the feeling feel less intense?

Put the book down and recall that same memory but feel the difference now, then open your eyes and read on.

Well done, so now you can take any memory, you can bring it to the present, and you can position it in the future, but this time you can change the way you feel about that memory so it doesn't cause you anymore pain. How many other memories have you buried that from time to time appear to stop you from doing things? You can do this with any memory, here are the steps again:

- o Recall the memory in your mind
- o Run it as a movie at normal speed
- o Run the movie backwards really fast, adding humour, funny faces, garbled noises of people speaking backwards and play the music in your mind loudly
- o Test how good you did by recalling that same memory again. What you are searching for is how different you feel now. It doesn't matter what the movie looks like, it's how you feel about it now

If you think you can't detect much difference in the way you feel after you have completed the exercise, close your eyes and reduce the size of the movie and move it away from you, until it is only a dot. Take a deep breath and blow it away until you can't see it, then check again. Remember this should only take you 20 seconds.

Do You Secretly Suffer From Shame, Fear And Guilt

A major cause of people not living an amazing life is their inability to remove shame, fear and guilt. Once we remove them you will attract so much more into your life.

Let me explain. Every single one of us on this planet can produce the feelings of guilt, fear or shame. All of us can and have at sometime in our lifetime. Now the problem is how do we get rid of these feelings and stop them resurfacing throughout our life?

We live in a world of opposites don't we? Where there is pleasure there is also pain. Love versus hate, happiness versus sadness. So we cannot ignore that there are always two sides to every feeling. We create them all and when it comes to shame, fear and guilt they can be very debilitating. People who come to see me for help often are carrying so much of these primary negative emotions that their lives have been devastated. They say they feel heavy. No wonder.

Now life does come with both sides of the coin, so you would agree I know that life can and often does throw at us challenging moments. Moments like death, divorce and other tragedies. However I also know and so do you that no matter how bad you can feel you somehow keep on going, even though you didn't know how. It's our built in survival system, the part of our make up that just keeps us upright and with a pulse.

We soldier on no matter what, we keep a stiff upper lip and we just get on with it. So if we can and do that anyway, I figured out a long time ago that we may as well feel different and change those awful feelings as soon as we can, rather than carry them through life.

There are two powerful ways to change these feelings. One is with your 7% conscious mind, that's the voice inside your head which is of course you talking to yourself. People often do this at night just when their head hits the pillow for sleep. An odd time you would think to go and have a chat to yourself.

The other way to change those negative feelings is with your 93% un-conscious mind. I will show you how later. When you use your 7% conscious mind you are using so little of your power it takes the trick of your mind to make it happen. Here's how you would go about it.

When you have something you feel ashamed, fearful or guilty about here is a great way to *shed those unwanted feelings* and at the same time change your perspective about it. I want you to write down 150 positive, powerful benefits that have resulted out of that past experience. So for example, if it was a relationship that ended and you felt guilty about what happened you would write down what you and the other person gained from that. *There is always some good* to come out of any life experience and this exercise helps you to think of the positives rather than the negatives.

I met a man who came to one of my "Amazing Life" day events and he told me he felt guilty for cheating on his partner. He said he couldn't live with the guilt anymore and he wanted to end his life.

Together we listed as many positive statements about what he could look at differently now. At first he couldn't find anything positive about it, however with some encouragement from me he began to tell me that there was a difference in his relationship now. He said he was closer to his partner now than ever before.

Their own intimacy was more profound and emotionally closer. The more he looked at the other side of what had happened, the more he began to heal. In two hours he cried, he laughed and by the time we had finished he had listed almost two hundred benefits of how such a terrible thing could have been a catalyst for his new feelings. He then told me he felt grateful for being able to have such a loving wife. Feeling grateful can move you to a calmer more soulful place.

No matter what happens in your life whether good or bad, you always need to look at both sides. When you do you can set yourself free from these terrible emotions. *You can always find something good in anything.* If you can't then you need to remember that life wasn't supposed to be just a walk in the park was it?

Here is your chance to do your list. No matter what your shame, fear or guilt is you can rid yourself of it right now, go to it and find some benefits in what happened. If it included another person or persons, include another 50 benefits for each person.

Your job now is to write your list, if you don't it's a waste of time reading the rest of this book, because everything else leads on from that list, so I urge you to do it. I'm told 90% of self-help readers don't complete the exercises in a book. I've included exercises that will have a profound affect on you and your loved ones, so please finish this chapter and take a moment to write your list.

I want you to think of your fear, shame or guilt and list any benefit you can think of now today, after the event. If you were hurtful to someone once, go back and now look at it differently. Now today it's different, because you said those things back then, the other person could now be wiser for your words to them.

What made you fearful back then won't bother you now when you look at it differently? False evidence is what fear is, so now you lived through that fear, it diminishes more and more.

You will be very surprised at how many you can list and how reading them will make you feel very different.

Drugs Are Killing Us

To live an amazing life you need to know with certainty that you can live it without anti-depressant drugs. I'm all for drugs that are required for medical problems, however I'll travel the world condemning the over prescribed abuse of anti-depressants.

It is without doubt impossible to live a truly amazing life while you or your children or loved ones are popping these highly addictive anti-depressants. Yes I do have a strong opinion on this and I'll let you know why.

I'm one of a few people in the world *that take people off these pills* and the industry that markets them for use doesn't like me. In fact I'd say they would love me to shut up and be quiet, not say another word about it. That will never happen.

Over all these years I have watched drug companies increase their market share and peddle their drugs in the sickness industry (that's where you go to the Doctor when you are sick) across to the wellness industry (that's where people go to prevent sickness).

Drug companies didn't like the fact that people were waking up and thinking to themselves they could prevent a lot of disease if they began to look after themselves better. The result of that decision which was lead by the "baby boomers" forced the drug companies to change direction and gain a foothold in the wellness industry.

So you make a decision to better look after your health and wellbeing, which means you do not need anti-depressants you need vitality and positive energy flowing in and around you.

Well if you are a drug company how on earth are you going to make any money from you? Do you see what has happened over the past ten years worldwide? There has been a massive increase in obesity and anti-depressant usage and they are related. When a person tricks their mind into thinking they are unhappy or depressed they normally turn to either food or anti-depressants or both.

It begins of course when an adult parent plays this depression trick in their mind and then forces that belief onto the child. First the poor self-pitying parents trick themselves into thinking he or she can't cope and calls a medical doctor for a non-medical item. The doctor, keen to up his chances of winning a trip to Hawaii for dispensing 8 million anti-depressants, obliges.

Now that the parent is numb to the world and addicted to these pills it's time to take care of all that noise and activity in that poor parents lives. Where shall they head next I hear you ask? The child. Yes we can't have a young child running all over the home full of energy and making noise, no way. Let's drug the child as well.

Today instead of allowing children to run around the world full of energy and expressing themselves, we drug them. Instead of honouring that child's talent for whatever they excel in, we stop them and if they fight back at us, we drug them. A child doesn't need motivation to go outside and play with their friends do they? They may need motivation to come in and wash their hands before dinner, but not to play.

Too many children are now taking Ritalin and other dangerous anti-depressant drugs all because the parent can't parent effectively

Just go back in time and think how the American Indians survived on the plains. Women living and roaming the country and giving birth on the road. Please, do you think an Indian woman told the Indian chief, "Hey I'm suffering from post natal depression can I rest a while?" No, they like other generations got on with it.

Today we are breeding a generation of soft limped pity me complainers

Today a child who plays a video game superbly well, needing no motivation and excelling using complicated brain functions required to play a video game, can't at that same moment be suffering from ADHD or ADD or any other bloody letter can they?

It's time *you* stopped listening to these pompous do-good *males* who miraculously somehow find the time to discover and publish these new disorders. God we even changed the bloody name of Manic Depression to Bipolar so we could market the drugs more effectively to a discerning public who didn't want to be associated with the word *manic*. However *bipolar* is? You work it out.

DON'T GIVE YOUR CHILDREN ANTI-DEPRESSANTS

It isn't high on their priority is it? I mean come on do you hear this across the world? "Mummy may I please have my anti-depressant so I don't feel like running outside and playing with my friends"?

If your child is on anti-depressants it's because of *your* priority, not theirs. So ask yourself why have you put your child on drugs, why? The answer will be your own fear, your own shame or your own guilt, which one drove you to do it. Fix it now before your child suffers even more. The child is ok, take a look at yourself and your life will awaken to a new meaning.

Warning

Don't stop the drug taking immediately. If your poor child or you have taken medication for a prolonged period it will need to be gradually reduced so the child and you don't suffer even more. Slowly does it. Seek professional help to get off them.

Negative Self Talk

You wake up in the morning and you start talking to yourself. We call that thinking by the way. For many people a busy chattering mind is what holds them back from living an amazing life. They are forever thinking negative thoughts (talking to themselves in a negative way). Here's a phrase people use in their head a lot and wonder why they worry so much. *"What if".*

Why in the world would someone ask that question? This is a question that habitually traps people into feeling negative. You need to understand that your mind needs time to rest along the journey. Being able to slow down your mind and filter those negative thoughts is very important.

So now you have a way of filtering negative thoughts you can now begin to learn *relax*. Everyone needs to learn to relax. A fast paced world and lifestyle tends to make people rush around, slow down and take moment to enjoy the present.

The Importance You Place On Things

You may not realise this but every decision you make and have made over your lifetime is made because of where you placed importance in that moment of your life. Your value of something or someone is how you make decisions. So we can agree that where you are in your life today is a direct reflection on where you have placed importance throughout your life.

If you are a parent right now to an infant baby it would be right to assume one of your highest priorities would be your child. So if you listed your top 20 priorities according to your own values, what would they consist of? Would number 2 on the list after the child be work or would it be the child's other parent? So unless you place a value on anything you won't make it a priority in your life. The infant child and the value you place on being a parent of that child forces you to move it to a higher priority.

I mean if the baby's nappy needs changing a mother will change it. She won't need external motivation to do it will she? The way you make decisions are based on what value you place on it so you can then make it a priority.

It's like someone who values money and building wealth, they have placed value on it and so therefore it's very high if not number one on their value list. Yet other people sometimes criticise people who place value on money as something evil or not honest. That's often because their own values and priorities are different.

In a relationship you can see the husband's range of boats, bikes, and other assortment of *boys toys*, perhaps mostly purchased with borrowed money. Those consumables are high on his lifestyle list, so he buys them no matter what they cost, he convinced himself he had to have them.

Meanwhile his wife comes to see me with a totally opposite view and value system in operation and argues with me that she is right and her husband is wrong, weird yes? Have you ever walked into your home and noticed your spouse has just purchased something, only for you to think what the @#$% is that for.

Take a look around you and everywhere you will see other people's values and priorities being acted out in their lives. What about the people who are labelled *neat freaks*? They have placed a value on being tidy, so it's high on their list.

What about people who sit watching television all day, some people call them lazy. Not at all, they have placed value and made it important for them to watch television all day, they are motivated to watch television all day. When you look at your world and the world around you it will become very obvious where people place their values. The nice thing about this is we all can and do choose where to place our values. The only problem comes when we want something we can't have. Like an amazing life full of wonderful relationships, wealth and doing the things you love to do. For some reason people don't understand what it is they are doing that isn't working for them. *You are about to find out why.* What do you value most in your life right now? Could you list the top ten things you value most in your life?

Write your list here :

1. _____

2. _____

3. _____

4. _____

5. _____

6. _____

7. _____

8. _____

9. _____

10. _____

As you look back at your list do you notice anything that stands out more than another? Do you know why you put your list together in that order?

This list was in your head and now it's down on paper or at least it should be. You have made many lists in your lifetime before and you will make other newer lists throughout the rest of your life. They change along your journey and when you write them down and look at them clearly they help you make life decisions.

I'm often asked why I am so motivated and committed and my answer is simple, I do what I love and I love what I do. You see no one has to get me to work on time. No one needs to motivate me to teach and help my students, clients and business associates.

It's as natural to me as a soccer ball is to the amazing David Beckham, one of the world's most popular soccer stars. If you asked David at the age of 12 what his top priority was, what do you think he would have said? Yes he would have said, "To be a professional footballer". Today however if you asked him to list his top 10 he would probably put his family at number one.

If you asked Bill Gates as a young student what his values were back then, what was his number one priority, what really excited him and motivated him, he may have said computers and creating software.

Mark Knopfler is one of the greatest guitar players on the planet so I wonder what he would have told you if you asked him what his values were as a teenager. Do you think he would have said making music or starting a band with his brothers?

Donald Trump, Warren Buffet, their values for building wealth is legendary. Warren read so many books at an early age that his popular saying has often been, "If you can't manage your emotions, you can't manage your money". How true it that? So if today right now I asked you to list your values, what is your top priority in your life today, what would it be?

When I do home visits I have the chance to see how other people live. They of course have no idea that what I see in their home and the way they live demonstrates clearly their own values in place right there and then.

One poor man had spent 4 years in his home unable to leave. Full of fear and shame he had the windows closed, curtains drawn and the house very dark. Within two hours he was out walking down the street next to me and today he leads an amazing life teaching my techniques to school children. His priorities when I made that home visit were easy to see. His only priority was his safety to stay indoors and of course he blew it out of proportion and ultimately believed the world was a dangerous place, thank god he doesn't now.

The wonderful thing about humans is that change is everywhere, it's inevitable and we can't even pretend to stop it. Some people even deny it or say they can't cope with change. Yet if you were to look through your old photo albums, then go to your mirror, I'm sure you are convinced that change is inevitable and has taken place.

So the message here is this. Your values and priorities change throughout your lifetime and within each area of your life. You need to understand what they are today so you can capitalise on them and use them to design your amazing life. Also you can change these values as well.

What Makes An Amazing Life

There are a number of areas that you need to look at in order for you to produce an amazing life. Having watched and given advice to many other people who live amazing lives, here are some of the answers they gave me to my question, what makes an amazing life?

- Freedom of choice
- Health
- Happiness
- Wealth
- Spiritual Connection
- To do what I love and love what I do
- To Be Motivated
- To have my own opinion accepted
- Vitality
- The love of a life long partner
- Knowing my own values
- Not being subservient to anyone
- Living without negativity
- A loving family

As you can see from such a varied list everyone has their own point of view. So it becomes what is important to you personally. No one else can create your life for you. No one can make this decision for you. So when you begin to think about designing your own amazing life, the areas that need your attention are:

- Personal Relationships (spouse/partner)
- Career (what you do that motivates you to go to work every day)
- Physical (looking after your body)
- Mental (how you manage your states)
- Financial (setting up wealth or poverty)
- Spiritual (your soul)
- Hobbies and Interests (what you do to balance your life)
- Social (how you interact with others)

As you read through this book I will mention these areas so you can have a clear picture of how you can live an amazing life. Many of the people I have met who live amazing lives did so because they found a cause greater than their own mortal self. A cause that was so great it took them far beyond what they would have done otherwise. Like for example this grandmother.

The Amazing Grandmother

This grandmother's grandson aged nine had been run over by a train and killed instantly on his way to school. The children who witnessed this tragic incident were in shock.

The entire district was stunned, the parents were in shock and everyone spent days and weeks in mourning over this very tragic incident. As the weeks rolled on everyone attempted to go back to their world and carry on, all except one person, the grandmother, who felt the heavy weight of guilt. Yes she blamed herself and felt guilty but it wasn't her fault. Eventually though she went on a quest that was to change her and many others lives.

This brave woman took on the railway authorities and made it her life long mission that railways and crossings across the country were to be safer and that rail lines and stations were all to get an upgrade. This devastating incident that killed her young grandson never left her, she battled governments and people all over the country and she would not stop until she had completed her mission. 5 years later the entire country had a safer rail network and it was all down to her.

Other countries contacted her for help and she ended up flying to many countries helping them stop more deaths on their railways. She went on to earn recognition for helping many countries save lives.

What makes an amazing life? The person, you make your amazing life. You make it by being tuned into the world in which you live in, not just the private world you set up for you. The world needs you just like it needed this grandmother, she made her life worthwhile in the face of tragedy. You don't need to wait for tragedy to strike to make your life amazing, start today.

Your Body Plays Tricks On You

When it comes to people and behaviour I have a confession to make, I love watching and modelling people. From the leading professionals in business, to great movie actors, to world-class sports stars, I've worked with them and I understand how they create their specific behaviours. So because I know that, I figure it would be a great idea to share that with you.

When we are born, we begin to grow into young people and then into adults. As we grow a few things begin to change along the way. The most important change begins early as an infant. You see, when you were laying in your dirty nappy screaming the house down, you didn't care about anyone else.

You didn't lay on the floor totally naked at 12 months old and scream out, "Mummy for God's sake woman put some clothes on me, I'm embarrassed".

No you couldn't because you couldn't speak, you didn't have a conscious mind, that's the voice inside your head that today as an adult can keep you awake at night. Do you know the one I mean?

As you developed and aged so too did your conscious mind through the use of language. You were then able to speak a few words and eventually learned that you could have an opinion. That's right you could now agree or disagree with other people and their opinions.

However just like before as you were growing up you also began to change other things. At a very young age you didn't really care about fear, dread, guilt or anxiety did you? Back then you wanted to be a fireman or a ballerina. All you wanted was to run and to play. As a young kid you even made up games and ideas about what to do to spend that hour you had with your best friend. Life then was truly amazing.

Then you went into your teenage years and didn't everything go wild then? Your hormones went one way and your anger the other. Your parents hid for cover as their little boy or girl emerged from the bedroom with steam erupting from their ears arguing about everything and anything.

It was in these impressionable and formative years that something amazing began to happen in your life. You began to play what I call *tricks of the mind* on yourself. Now earlier on in your young life you did the same but it was fun and you enjoyed the trick. You may have imagined you were a cowboy or a great dancer. However as a teenager you began to view your world differently. As you matured so too did your ability to convince yourself that what happened to you in terms of how you felt, you thought was real.

You see you became enlightened and as a result you were able to convince yourself about all manner of things.

Your body began to change and so too did your opinion of yourself.

One of the major things that happened when you were a teenager was your need to fit in with a group. Being in the right group at school was very important to you back then. If you were left out of the group you would feel sad, however if included you felt as though you belonged. When you look back today ask yourself this question. What group were you so desperate to be in or stay in? If you have school age children now understand that this is their number one priority right now.

So if you understand that when you were a teenager you could trick yourself into believing you needed to fit in, today as an adult you need to be aware that you can still do the same. The major problem is people often trick themselves into thinking something is real when it isn't. That's the power of thought.

For example, a person walked into my office and said, "Patrick, I have Anxiety". I replied, "Cool, I have chocolate". What's happened to the language here?

People today think they *have something.* That's because people have to find a label for a feeling. If they don't give it a name the drug companies can't sell you the drug to trick you into thinking you feel okay again.

Let's take anxiety. For any human being to begin to feel anxiety about anything they first have to set up a belief that allows their body to feel anxious, and they need to make sure they know what feeling anxious actually feels like.

How do they know they are anxious by the way? How do they know when to display the anxiety or how do they know when not to display it? How many times has a person who says they suffer from anxiety *forgotten* to display it? I ask that question to people every day. I say what happens if you forget to be anxious and they look at me kind of weird looking and can't answer. Anxiety like all other feelings appears in the body.

The moment your body feels anything other than peace and comfort, you have played a trick on yourself and your body is letting you know

I'll ask an anxiety sufferer, "How often do you feel anxious?" The normal answer, "Well *it* comes and goes". So now it's an IT. IT comes and goes, what comes and goes? The IT, where did the IT come FROM? The IT in fact is the trick the person played in their mind.

Try this as you read along with me please. Think of something from your past that really is not very nice. It could be a trauma or a bad relationship that ended. Anything will do as long as it's from your past. Go ahead and think for a moment, I'll stop writing and wait for you.

Good, so now that you have that memory in your mind, how does it make you feel right now? Do you notice how your body has changed? Where do you feel this? In the throat, in the chest, in the tummy, the hands, where does it get you?

By now you would have felt a difference in your body. If you haven't I'm guessing you are either on anti-depressants, didn't do the exercise or you have an over active conscious mind (voice) in which case you should tell yourself to be quiet next time we do a technique please.

So by now you are getting the idea that you make up your own behaviour and feelings internally with your mind. You use language and you talk to yourself, and yes I know some people do it too much and can't switch off. When you talk to yourself your other mind, the sub-conscious mind is listening and openly receiving everything in great detail. It doesn't argue with your other mind, it just accepts it all as real.

That's what is so incredible about your mind. You can tell yourself anything you want, then with a trick of the mind create a chemical response in your body and your behaviour is formed.

In Australia I've become the guy to go to if you can't climb up the Sydney Harbour Bridge. This reputation was created as a result of my TV appearances demonstrating how quickly I can get someone who thinks they can't do it, to actually do it and have a great time. The downside to this is that every celebrity arriving from overseas that is afraid to climb the bridge, has their agent call me. They, just like you, can trick their mind into thinking they can't climb the bridge, yet they know they should be able to, but their body won't let them. It's a trick.

The reason we know so much about the human mind and body now is that for years we have been treating people with irrational fears, which we call Phobia's.

People worldwide have fears of heights, snakes and spiders to name the popular one's. However when you do my work I get to play with the stupid Phobia's, one's like fear of cotton wool or fear of people. Believe it or not I have cured plenty of celebrities worldwide of their fears of stage or fear of failure. Anyone can trick himself or herself.

By the way everyone (and I mean everyone) on earth plays this trick of the mind on themselves. For example a smoker tricks their mind to believe they need a cigarette every hour or so. The fun thing now is that when people come to me to quit, it only takes a few minutes rather than the old fashioned way of weeks and months. Once the smoker understands how they tricked themselves in the first place they soon work out that all they really needed every hour or so was a big deep breath. They just created the illusion they needed to suck poison every hour.

So the world has 7 billion people who all trick themselves into feeling emotions that are not real. Once the feelings enter their bodies people think that they now have a disorder and it's off to the Medical Doctor for some drugs. Weird world we live in when uneducated people go to a medical doctor for a non-medical problem.

Here's how all people with a pulse make their behaviour. We think (talk to ourselves) and then we pass the information onto and into our sub-conscious mind. That's the mind that doesn't argue with you. Once the chemicals have reached there we begin to feel them in our body, where we have to name it, so it becomes an *it* with a name, like anxiety.

Then we complete the transition by believing we can't change the feelings ever. I'll also show you how tricking your mind stops you from living a truly amazing life in the first place.

What Are Your Needs

Here is a list of the most commonly known needs.

Certainty

Every human has needs. You have a need for certainty in your life. If you go too long without certainty you may go and look for certainty in the form of comfort and short-term gratification in alcohol, drugs, sex or just switching off from the family or world.

Uncertainty or Variety

When you have too much certainty you become bored and without realising look again for uncertainty. Your level of certainty is different than other peoples so don't be surprised that your level of stress and that of your loved ones are not the same.

Significance

Everyone at some point in there life has felt the need to feel important. It could be as a spouse, a parent, a family member or even at work. You have deep inside you the need to be significant, don't ignore it as this need brings with it amazing life changes.

Connection

Once again these needs blend into each other. If you become too significant then it is difficult to connect with people. People want to feel connected and to do so often means realising that we are all similar in what makes us tick. A feeling of connection in all areas of your life is important.

Growth

When a person plateaus they feel like they have stopped growing as a person. If you stop you actually fall behind the rest. As the world keeps evolving, so too does your need to continue to grow and discover how much you still have to learn.

Contribution

Another deep need humans have is this need to make a contribution. This is far and above what we do with and in our lives. Contributing to the world or your local community is something people have done since the dawn of time. If you haven't made your contribution yet then start today and enjoy the benefits. Yes there are more needs that could be listed here but what I wanted to establish for you was the biggest need, which is to create a balance in your life that provides you with an enjoyable way to live an amazing life. When you keep balanced you live with little or no stress and fulfil all of these needs often.

The Power Of Feeling Truly Grateful

When I talk about a person's perception, I mean the view or opinion they take on a certain thing, person or anything they wish to have a view on. It's their personal perception.

As free humans we all have the ability to view our own personal world and the real world as we see fit. A person living on the streets with only a newspaper and a park bench for shelter may view their world differently than you view yours.

Yet I have met thousands of people over my 30 plus years of teaching that no matter where they live still find a way to complain. These people come under the label of ungrateful. No matter where or what they have it still wouldn't make them grateful.

So much of my work with people is to teach them how to be grateful again, because all of us were once grateful. That gratefulness was born in all of us no matter our colour or creed. Yet for many the life journey they have experienced has altered their own perception of how to be grateful.

Have you ever felt sad when something bad happened to others? Then followed that feeling up with feeling grateful that either it wasn't as bad as you first thought, or that you felt relieved it didn't happen to you or your loved ones?

If we drive past a motor accident on the road, we slow down to see, then make sure we don't know the car and sometimes hold our breath when we recognise one of the cars involved in the accident. If we are wrong and it's no one we know we feel grateful, or if you don't here's lesson one, feel grateful.

When we start from a place of feeling grateful about who we are and where we are in our life it prevents powerful negative emotions taking over and it allows our heart and soul to be reached

A person with too much time on their hands will often arrive in my office complaining of depression or anxiety. What do you think they think about most? Would it be great wealth, how they will make a contribution to the world or maybe help out in their local community? No these people think of all the bad things they can about their past, present and then finish the thought pattern with going to the future and putting negative thoughts in that too. Then they come and see me for help.

As you can see it's impossible to feel grateful and at peace with your life if you keep spending it thinking about negative memories or fearful futures. These people view their world sadly and with unhappiness most of the time, yet as you have already discovered so quickly, we can all change the way we feel fast.

So let me take you through how someone who has a very negative view of their world does it. First because they have plenty of time their mind wanders to negative thoughts. Mostly thoughts like what they don't have in their lives. In order for them to trick their mind into believing this negative thought they have created some form of *void* in order to tell themselves to feel negative.

For example if they were thinking how they have a lack of self-confidence, how do they know that to be true? I mean don't they first have to believe they haven't enough confidence? In order to do that they convince themselves they have a lack of something, in this case confidence. It could be anything they trick their mind into thinking they have a lack of. Only then can they tell themselves through the thoughts and then the chemical change in the body that they are now suffering a lack of self-confidence and therefore it would be impossible to feel grateful at the same moment.

So, as you can see to feel grateful you need to be able to access that feeling and access it as often as possible until it becomes a habit. Thankfully us humans are built to create habits, some better than others. Smoking is the type of habit you can't do at the same time as tricking your mind into thinking you are a smart person. You can't be intelligent and smoke at the same moment can you?

When you come from a place of gratitude you have the foundation for an amazing life because it prevents negative thoughts getting in your way. Now I'm not suggesting for one moment that we don't all become unhappy or sad at some stage throughout our life. What I am saying is don't make it a habit, don't have a personal view of your life that is negative no matter what you feel like. Remember we can change our feelings.

Turning A Perceived Loss Into A Transition

I had a man come to see me and tell me he couldn't get past the fact he had lost his marriage, it was over. He had spent almost two years trying to get over the breakup. Now for anyone on earth a marriage breakup has to be a terrible thing to go through, however if people walk in my office I figure it's time they moved on. So here is how I helped this sad man feel grateful.

"Did you once love each other", I asked. "Yes we did" he replied with tears rolling down his face. "Did you have any children together?" I asked. "Yes we did", he again replied. "Did you have plenty of fun times as a family?" I asked. His reply was the same. As his tears of sadness kept flowing, soon to be joined by my own tears if I wasn't careful, I began his transformation.

Slowly at first I made comments about how the marriage must have been so special. I also mentioned that I was sure that even though he and his ex wife were no longer together they would always be in a relationship being the best parents they could be. He began to tell me that he thought she was not a good mother. I quickly reminded him that his opinion was only according to him and that it was made from an unhappy heart. He agreed, wiping away his tears.

As I carried on my comments to him (he had no idea of course what I was doing) I asked him to begin to think of all the good times he'd had with his children in the past and then I asked him how often he saw his children now. Not very often was his answer. I asked him if he thought it was his duty to see his children as much as possible because even in his pain his children needed him now more than ever. He agreed. *The quality and type of questions I asked is the key here!*

He mentioned his 18 year-old daughter and I quickly asked him if it would be he who walked this daughter down the wedding aisle. He smiled for the first time and my time to teach this man gratitude was upon us. I told him a story about how I helped a man once in a similar position, in fact that year alone I saw over 340 men who had lost their marriages also. He was very surprised, which helped unlock his sadness and allowed us to release it.

I told him I had helped this man by asking him to list as many benefits as he could think of now that the marriage was over. This man I was sat next to who was an hour earlier crying was now writing down benefits of his marriage ending instead of feeling sorry for himself. As he listed them he even told me they used to argue so loud and often during the last 5 years of their marriage they should have broken up earlier.

I've heard that so many times of course, but as this man was listing all these benefits he wasn't realising that every time he listed another he was giving his brain and his neuro pathways a new reason to feel grateful. By the time we were finished this man had a new life to look forward to. He was smiling and looking forward to calling his children. He had in fact written so many reasons as to why it was a good thing to end the marriage that he had now convinced himself. All I had to do was clean up some shame and guilt he had over some things which were very easily collapsed. When the why is large enough, the how to move forward takes care of itself.

He left feeling grateful because he had now learned from his relationship. He had wonderful children and he had a new perspective on his own life. Whatever grief you have or had in your life, write down at least 150 benefits as to why it was a good thing. Yes of course I know that sounds ridiculous, I've grief counselled thousands of people who have lost loved ones, many in terrible circumstances, including suicide, bombings and other tragic circumstances.

However I do know one thing. After 30 years of helping people overcome their worst nightmares, in the end they will end the grief, the pain and the anger. Once I have them through that I only have to repair the fences of gratitude. So as you can see there is no loss or gain, there is only a transition.

How Suggestible Are You?

Living an amazing life means you will share the world with others. One amazing lesson I teach in my workshops and private sessions is how to discover the *Suggestibility* of the type of person you are communicating with. When you communicate with others you often find yourself attempting to get your point of view across or attempting to understand the other persons point of view, don't you?

So understanding this area of communication is very important as you and the other people in your world often like to suggest things to each other. I'm going to show you how people get it wrong and then show you how to get it right. I'll put the link to the video of this at the end so you can watch me explain it.

There are three types of people when we talk in terms of suggestibility; I am going to focus on the primary two. The Physical Suggestible and the Emotional Suggestible. Either can be male or female, there is no discrimination.

A Physical Suggestible person is someone who doesn't use their emotions openly in their communication and tends to keep their feelings to themselves most of the time. Nothing wrong with that at all, it's an observation and one you need to understand.

The Emotional Suggestible on the other hand displays their emotions freely in their communications. Once again nothing wrong with showing emotions, I just want you to become more aware.

Now why am I telling you this? Because when you understand these differences you'll dramatically improve all of your relationships in all areas of your life. To build an amazing life you do it with people, so this is very powerful and not many people even know about this. Now you do, so use it. As a Hypnotist I know the value in understanding this because if I am to offer help, I do it in the way of *offering positive suggestions*.

An Emotional Suggestible person will *never* take one suggestion only because the biggest fear for an emotional suggestible person is a *Loss of Control*. So therefore if you are always suggesting only the one thing, if he or she perceives it to threaten their major fear, they will reject it instantly. Often this may be followed with a very loud discussion that could almost pass as an argument or eventually even warfare.

So if your partner is an Emotional Suggestible human, offer many different solutions and if you can stay away from suggesting anything that may lead them to that major fear of losing control, even better.

Now the Physical Suggestible major fear is the *Fear of Rejection*. It is just as difficult to discover and many couples over the years have been shocked when after only speaking for a few minutes I interrupt them and do a perfect description of each of them and their traits, and then list the top 5 things where the marriage is failing. Yet if they knew about these suggestible states we often inherit, life would be easier and perhaps even happier rather than competitive all the time.

With a Physical Suggestible person if you are about to give them a suggestion, keep it short, give them just one option, not several like the Emotional Suggestible and the Physical Suggestible person will normally accept the suggestion and move on. So don't keep on about it, deliver your suggestion and that's it.

So an Emotional Suggestible person shows their emotions freely. They need several options and none preferably that lead to him or her believing they will lose control.

The Physical Suggestible will often accept one suggestion if it's kept short (especially if it's a male). Remember when you argue with a Physical Suggestible person if you threaten them and they believe they will be rejected by you, all hell can break out. It could be sulking and quiet or rage and screaming, so learn what works, instead of reoffending with what doesn't work.

Here is an example of how *not* to make a suggestion to an Emotional Suggestible person:

"I think we should go to the movies at the weekend".

This type of suggestion will have the Emotional Suggestible person thinking about their lack of control concerning the movies.

However if you phrase it another way like:

"I was thinking about the weekend and what we could do. Now there is the bowling alley or water polo or we could pop into the movies, I'd prefer the movies but what about you, I don't really mind either way?" Notice how I provided options, kept the questions less threatening and made it easy for them to choose.

The quality of your life is brought about by the quality of the questions you ask

The Physical Suggestible needs phrasing that doesn't move them towards a feeling of rejection. So don't suggest things where they may feel threatened or rejected.

This example is from a real case so pay attention to what happened to each of them. See if you can pick which one is the emotional and which one is the physical. A couple decided to go to a concert. On the way there they were both happy and excited.

They parked their car in the long distance car park like many others and went by free mini bus to the arena. There were dozens of buses taking the people to the arena. After the concert they began to walk outside and prepare to get the minibus back to the car park. Everything was perfect up until then. Suddenly the wife grabbed the husband by the wrist as if her life depended upon it and dragged him running up a hill towards one of the minibuses.

The husband was totally surprised by his wife's sudden movement towards the bus and reacted by saying, "Wait a moment we can catch the next bus there are plenty of buses coming every minute". As he was trying to get the wife to stop running after the bus, she began to scream, "Hurry up, or we will miss this bus". As the husband was hauled into the bus catching his breath he became very angry, even with a bus full of people watching and listening he began to tell his wife off for making him run up a hill after a bus. He was becoming more and more angry and by the time they had reached their car, the wife decided she wouldn't get in. The night ended badly.

Now what just took place to cause this and can you pick which one was the Emotional Suggestible and which one was the Physical Suggestible? In their session with me we identified the following:

The wife was the Physical Suggestible and as she stood waiting for the bus she, like all humans went into a daydream, every nine minutes we all go daydreaming. When she woke up she looked up and saw a bus moving away from her. This immediately went to her core fear of *rejection* and upon realising this she panicked and grabbed the husband and chased the bus. *Rejection*. I know you are probably thinking, Patrick come on now how does a back of a bus make someone feel rejected. But understand this, these ingrained fears are habitual, you are not even aware of them you just act on them out of habit and impulse.

So the husband was the Emotional Suggestible and once he had believed he had *lost control* he also panicked, then out of habit he responded with emotion to what took place. This couple ended the session laughing because once they understood this concept they talked about all the other times they had been upset with each other. Relationships are like that, you do very often end up in an argument and you can't even remember the topic or how it began. This is a wonderful way to identify yourself and who you are. Think about all the other people in your life and work out which one they are and begin to communicate like I have suggested. You will discover your communication skills will improve dramatically. Why? Because they will love to talk about all the things that are important to them and at the end say how great it was talking to you!!!!

If you want to become truly effective at communicating make sure you also understand that not everyone on the planet is interested in your top ten priorities or values. Other people have their own priorities, their own interests and like you they also want someone to listen to them. You can become the best communicator (listener) in the world by knowing this. Now go and listen to someone.

The reason you need to improve your communication skills with people is they are the ones who you live with, sell to, socialise with and ultimately may even attend your funeral. Think about it, what is more important in your life than being able to fully communicate with people you want in your life? You can repair broken relationships now that you know how to communicate more effectively. No more competition between you and others. Now you can feel grateful and understand that other people have the right to an opinion and you welcome their opinion. By changing the way you communicate you will discover even more about people. They will love you for it. Here is the video link

The Law Of Attraction

This law of attraction phrase has become very popular and like everything in our world everyone has an opinion on it. Here is how patients, my clients and I use this universal law. I believe that the law of attraction basically states that what we think about most will be attracted into our reality. My understanding is that no matter whether you think positive or negative, whenever you give thought to something or someone, that will be attracted into your reality.

The reason I keep saying into your reality and not into your life will become more evident as you read the rest of this book. So we can now think about what we want most and then have it come to us. If it's that easy why doesn't everyone on the planet have an amazing life?

Every day of my working life I see people using the law of attraction in their life. Let me give you some examples. Gerry is a man aged 52 and has visited me from time to time over the past few years. Instead of hiring me as his coach, Gerry preferred to just book in and see me whenever he thought he should. So once a year or maybe twice some years, Gerry would walk in and have a chat with me about how much money he still doesn't have. I would ask him if he had made his millions of dollars yet and his reply would be, "I'm just making enough to pay the bills thankfully".

Now here was a man who was intelligent and worked all his life, but still didn't understand that he had literally programmed his mind to let him know how thankful he was that he made *just enough money* to pay his bills. Because he told himself the same story year in year out that all he could do was just make enough, his mind helped him achieve just that and no more than that. How was Gerry ever going to build great wealth if his own thoughts and now his habitual programming only allowed him to earn just enough to pay bills? He was indeed using the law of attraction to attract into his life just enough money to pay bills.

A woman used to come and see me under similar circumstances as Gerry every now and then. She would always turn up when her life was a drama. She would go away for a year or two, create massive drama and emotional pain for her and others then come and tell me about it. I would give her some tips on how *not* to repeat it and after two sessions not see her again for a few years until, yes you guessed it, she had created another drama. She kept saying to herself that she would never find the man of her dreams. Obviously she was using the law of attraction perfectly in terms of what she thought about most would happen, however it was all the things she didn't want.

To make matters really dramatic she would go away and pick men who would hit her and abuse her. All this was done because all she wanted was a family. The last time I heard she had given up on finding the man of her dreams and was pregnant again for the fifth time in her single life.

These examples and thousands more explain one major thing to me. Be very careful what you think about and continue to think about. These two people kept thinking about what they *didn't want* instead of thinking about what they *did want*. When you next talk with people listen to how they use the law of attraction. You will be amazed at how often you will hear someone say out loud what they don't want to happen.

For example:
- Oh the wedding is only 6 months away I so don't want to be big
- I hope she doesn't call me today
- I need a job soon or I'll lose my home

When they do this and continue to do this they attract it into their reality and it becomes real. I've listened to mothers watching their children play on a swing. One mother says hold on tight and the other mother says be careful you don't fall off that swing.

My mother was Irish and she would say to me, "Don't run or you could fall over and break your leg and if you do don't come running to me for help".

So how do you use this powerful internal programmable language pattern? First I need to let you know that to learn to use this law to your advantage it will either take many days, months or even years of practice or you could learn it as fast as one heartbeat. The choice will be yours. If I can I want to convince you how important this skill is and if I can I want to teach you how to develop your skills. However, before I do that you will need to decide if this is going to be important enough to you. I know that humans only do things when they feel it is important to them, so if this becomes important enough to you I know you will develop these powerful skills. Here is how I help people transform their lives fast by using the law of attraction.

Step 1 - Split your day into segments.

One of the biggest problems for people is keeping control of their own thoughts. We have so many thoughts to deal with every minute, hour and day that if we have a bad day, it will be because our thinking wasn't in order. People get overwhelmed when their thoughts are running wild inside their head.

So I use this method to help organise and keep control of my thoughts. I wake up and as I open my eyes this is my first segment. Now in this sleepy warm comfortable state lying in bed I begin to say thank you. I might say it fifty times or more, I just keep saying thank you and then I begin to add things and names to what I'm saying thank you for. Like perhaps adding my family names and friends and the weather or the flowers. It doesn't matter what I'm thankful for I just developed this segment because it is the beginning of a day. I don't know if it will be my last on this earth, so I am thankful for it. The more I say thank you the more I begin to feel grateful.

My next segment is interaction at breakfast and preparing for the day. My next segment is travel to work or wherever I am going in the morning. My next would be commencement of work. So split your day up and section off times in that day where you have time to set in motion positive thoughts about what you want most to happen. Then you can make your thoughts meaningful and intentional for what you want in that moment and concentrate your power on that and nothing else. This is very good for helping you stay in the present moment and enjoy feeling amazing.

Step Two – Deliberate Creation

Once you have completed the previous step you can now focus all of your intention on creating your amazing life. When you deliberately create thoughts that say what you want most in your life and you are specific in what it is you truly want, your body provides the emotion needed to make you feel it.

A thought may linger with you a while then disappear, however when you think of something and then feel a positive emotion towards that thought it becomes real for you. That's how some people scare themselves. They think of what they don't want, and then imagine how bad it will feel and before they know it, they feel it.

If we were to take those previous examples and change them to what they really were trying to say they might be phrased like this:

- Oh the wedding is only 6 months away, I so don't want to be big. (Negative)
- By the time my wedding day arrives I want to be a size (insert dress size you desire) and feel calm relaxed and slim. (Positive)

Can you see the difference in the way I have changed this thought to something more positive. It's what every bride would want.

- I hope she doesn't call me today (Negative)
- Today I want a day where I will have few, if any interruptions (Positive)
- I need a job soon or I'll lose my home (Negative)
- My home is safe because I want to get a job in the next two weeks. (Positive)

In this example I have also included a timeframe to help me move my powerful attraction to a job opportunity within a time period. Also notice that I didn't use the word *need*. The word need is different than want. Use the word want and begin to want more in your life. Wanting a better education or more money is a positive thought. Keep using phrases that explain your wants in a positive term. Here is an exercise that I urge you to do. It is also very useful to do this a few times a year, just to check you are on track.

Draw a line from top to bottom on an A4 piece of paper creating two columns. On the left hand side of that line write down the following words: *I Don't Want* and then on the right hand side write down *I Want* . Now go to the left hand side and list all the things you don't want to happen in your life. Really include as many as you can. Don't leave anything out. If you need another page go for it. Once you have listed all the things you don't want, go to the right hand side of the page and take the first one you don't want and change the language and write it in the positive, just like I showed you earlier.

Your job is to list everything you don't want and then list them in the opposite way. Make sure you do this exercise, it will open up so much more in your life when you do this. You will attract so much more and it will arrive so much faster than you first imagined. I've had people email me saying they did this exercise and within a few days something profound happened. So please do this wonderful exercise.

When you have that done go and stand in front of a mirror with your list and say out loud the list of positive intentions you want. Make sure you say each one with emotion. If you do this exercise correct you will begin to tear up and become emotional. That's perfect by the way. I want you to read each of the things you want in your life and do it with power. Yes you will cry and as you cry you are releasing all those negative feelings you have captured by thinking about what you didn't want, rather than what you really wanted. Enjoy this very personal and powerful experience. You will be well on your way to a life long habit of always thinking what you truly want in your life rather than what you don't want. I devised this exercise a few years ago and the response has been amazing.

Step Three – Law Of Allowing

Every one on the planet has the free right to an opinion. I hope you agree with that statement. You have a right to your opinion yet when you attempt to deliver that opinion to some people they often resist or even disagree with it don't they? Have you ever wondered why so many people argue in the world? Well it's because they don't understand this law.

You see the law of allowing means that you want to allow others to be, say and have what they want. Just like the law of attraction says what you want most will arrive. The problem for many is that once another person arrives with a different opinion than them, they begin to feel negative towards the other person and/or the opinion being stated. If this happens to you then you are not allowing, and the easiest way of using the law of allowing is to go back and focus on what it is you *want* most in your own life.

If you keep to your focus of thinking what you want instead of what you don't want then the law of allowing is very easy and powerful. I meet people every day that spray their pain all over my office. They are hurting bad and most of them say it's because of what others have said or done to them. How did this arrive in their lives? They attracted it. Every human on earth is entitled to a free opinion. It doesn't mean you need to react to that opinion in a negative or positive way at all. You just need to allow that other person to voice their opinion and accept they are allowed to have one.

My Awakening

I was on location in the far northwest outback of Australia, 300 kilometres inland from the town of Broome, Western Australia where the roads are red dust.

I'd already been invited to go and teach there the year before and had agreed to go back. It was a very long and tiring journey and once in this community you were completely cut off from the rest of the world. The community was made up of 99.9% Aboriginals and a few white people.

My job was to teach the youth of the community and to help them reduce the cases of petrol sniffing, alcohol abuse and youth suicide. This community had a reputation for those things and more. Recently there had been a couple of youth suicides and the township wasn't at ease at all. I could feel the tension as I walked through the red dusty streets. It was very sad to know that young people were ending their lives.

My 10 days there this time included a film crew who were producing a documentary of my work. Once I began my program of work though I soon realised that classroom lectures and live demonstrations were probably not going to work. I needed something else. That night I went out alone without the film crew to talk to the elders who told stories throughout the night about how the community was once a proud and popular town. They used to grow food and breed horses and sell them on to neighbouring townships across the outback of Australia.

I'd been listening to these elders for hours and noticed how proud they sounded as they recapped the good old days. I also noticed the look on the faces of some of the young boys who were listening intently to the stories. It reminded me of my own childhood where we would huddle around the big open fire listening to all the funny Irish folklore stories.

The next day I woke up with a voice in my head saying, "Horses, horses". So I organised as many 4 wheel drive vehicles as possible and loaded up all the young people of the town that were supposed to be sat in a classroom and headed out into the desert. I was about to take this town back to their roots, we were about to go and capture wild horses, the legendary wild Australian Brumbies.

As we approached the rocky outcrop where the elders said horses would be, my guide for the day came over the radio saying he had spotted the horses. He wanted us all to help him drive them all the way back to town, where the rest of the townsfolk were busy building a temporary coral.

We spent over three hours chasing these wild horses. Every time we thought we got close the stallion would head his herd the other way. A few vehicles didn't quite make it and I was lucky not to have disappeared down a cliff face that suddenly appeared. The hazard of driving at

70 kilometres an-hour in a rough terrain desert attempting to catch 30 horses that just didn't want to be caught can be a little scary, but great fun, the young people loved it. Eventually the horses slowed down and we were able to get them into the pens to water and feed them. The whole town was out and cheering. The teenagers who helped round them up were sitting on the fences clapping and cheering, it was as if we had all gone back in time and we felt this powerful feeling run through us all.

My last few days were spent going over how they would now relaunch their community and everyone wanted to be involved. I had over 500 people all busy again instead of sitting around doing nothing. It was an overwhelming success, something that will remain with me forever.

However this is why I'm letting you know about this. One of the elders came up to me as I was about to board my plane and began to thank me. He said, "Dr Joe (that's my Australian Aboriginal Name) you helped my people again, I thank you. I wish to help yours also". As he finished speaking he put out his arm to shake hands with me.

I leaned forward and held out my hand to his and as he closed his hands over mine I felt what I would best describe as a *mild lightening bolt* shoot up my arm. At the time of course I didn't think much of it, thinking it was my boots rubbing on the red dust. I said goodbye and he looked at me kind of strange and smiled. He must have been well into his 90's and I returned my thanks and boarded my plane.

As I landed in Sydney Airport I went over to my car and began the drive home. Halfway home I began trembling, my entire body began to shake so much I had to stop the car. My mouth went dry, I shook all over and all I could see was this purple colour all over me. Every time I moved my hand or arm or leg there was this purple streak following me.

After what felt like hours I stopped shaking and composed myself enough to call someone I thought might know what had just happened. He didn't help much but gave me a telephone number of a woman who could help. She told me I had a *spiritual awakening*, she said I must have been doing a lot of healing in order to bring out such colours. I hadn't realised then but for the past ten days I'd been healing many people. As I drove home all I could think about was how the community had changed so much and I had the opportunity to help them, I felt very humbled and proud. It was and still is the weirdest drive home from an airport I have ever had. By the time she had finished telling me all about what was happening to me my fear turned to excitement.

Like any excited Philosopher I began to search the world for answers to questions about colours and Auras and anything I could study. The first year was a real problem because every book I read on the subject gave a different interpretation on what the colours meant. So instead of wasting another year reading book after book on the subject I decided to do my own research. Every patient, client and celebrity that I worked with over the next two years I kept a record of the colour aura they had when they arrived in my office and the colour when they left.

Ninety percent of the time the colour people arrived with was red and the same percentage left with the colour changed to gold. So having discovered that I went one step further. I then wanted to know what happened with their aura colour with each technique I would teach them to perform. Sure enough another pattern appeared. Each of my techniques changed their colours.

So then I had an even faster way of helping people. I was already fast at curing people but with the aid of seeing a persons aura colours I could pinpoint a problem without asking the patient and then offer a technique that immediately cured their issue fast. It was a real breakthrough in my work.

Spirituality Or Intuition

For some people the word spirituality conquers up religion, however in this text religion is not what I am teaching. In this chapter you may find a new understanding especially if you talk to yourself a lot of the time.

Here's how I understand spirituality, it may not be what others think, but it works for me. I have a set of guardians and guides (spirits) that look out for me and protect me. Some people call them Angels. Whatever you call them they are mostly past relatives of yours and others who come along to help you. Also these spirit guides change throughout your lifetime. Currently one of my guides is St Peter. Jennifer, who I see from time to time confirmed this recently as she was told by him that he walked with Jesus. Apparently he is here to help me with my writing, so stay tuned for many more books, reports and written guides by me.

My mother, who passed away back in the 80's, is my main guardian. Recently that changed because she moved over to look after my brother who was told he was gravely ill. Sadly my brother passed away on the 8th November 2012. My Father also passed away on the 8th November, but eleven years ago. My grandfather who died before I was born looks out for me at the time of writing this book. I also have another guide who I call Ben as he is my protector and is massive.

I understand spirituality this way. When I use my intuition, I'm tapping into a higher level of consciousness. I'm listening to my team of guides and my guardians. That is my understanding of my intuition. My guardians know and protect me all the time but let me tell you it has taken me years to get used to it and even allow myself to open up and let it be part of my life.

One night while I was driving home I had this voice in my head telling me to slow down, drive slower. I'm a male, so of course I didn't listen to the voice until it sounded like my mother's voice telling me off, to which I took my foot off the throttle and as I did my back wheel snapped off from my car. The car finally stopped about half a metre from a tree. If I had not slowed down I would have hit the tree and would most definitely have died. Once again my mother came to my rescue. The tow truck driver couldn't believe the back wheel could have snapped like it did and took a long time getting the car up onto his truck.

By the way, this type of occurrence has already happened in your life (not the car accident). The simple ones like the phone rings and you pick it up and it is someone you had just been thinking of. How do you explain that? I explain it by saying my team of spirit guides and guardians are with me in the form of being my intuition. I listen to them now as they guide my life decisions with me.

How many times have you not acted on your intuition? I meet people all the time who don't use their intuition. A wife that knew something was wrong, felt it, heard words in her head, and yet did nothing about it only to discover her husband had three other women in three other cities. She knew something wasn't right, but didn't act on it. Her guides were desperately trying to let her know of his deceit.

When you don't act on your intuition you pay the price. You can't live an amazing life without listening to your intuition. So now you can totally understand how your intuition works for you. Every time you go against what you deep down know, then you are not listening to your guides.

Imagine you are out alone late at night. There are two roads leading to where you want to go. One is the long way around but well lit with cars and people walking. The other way is much shorter but dimly lit, you hear the sound of bottles breaking and loud voices. Which way would you walk? Your intuition tells you which way you should go, but some people don't listen or act on their intuition.

When you learn to communicate with your spirit guides your world opens up even more. You have more freedom and more appreciation of life and the world around you. You also have far more control on how to plan and live your amazing life, but the biggest change for me was my certainty. I always thought I felt certain when making decisions or helping patients but since I openly accepted and speak to my guides I have become even more certain.

With this ability to listen to yourself and act on your *gut feeling* means you are listening to your intuition and not tricking your mind negatively. I say things to patients these days and they look stunned because I know so much about them. If they accept spirituality then I explain I am speaking to their guides. If they are not into it then I tell them I just guessed.

Using your intuition is one of the most important skills you need to learn if you want to live an amazing life. By using your intuition much more than ever before you will in fact prevent others in your life dominating what you do and what you think you should do. No one has the right to dictate to others what they should think, feel or be.

I urge you to tap into your own intuition. Remember don't go and get a psychic reading, you don't need anyone pretending they know what is going to happen in your future. Just begin to read and learn how your guides work for you and be amazed.

Of course it helps when every day people in need come in to see me and I can practice hour after hour with my clients. Some days I'll talk to a dozen different clients, but also chat to dozens of their spirit guides, so my office is often very crowded. I've learned that you need to be respectfully forceful with spirit guides otherwise they begin to learn that they can just hang around and listen in to others issues. I clear my room of spirits and negative energy after every session these days, then the only guides that come through are the ones my next client brings with them.

Let me give you a really small example of how I use my guides. When I am about to enter a car park I ask my guides to find me the nearest parking spot to the entrance. Every time I ask one suddenly appears. My family laugh every time I do it and of course some of them don't believe in this and of course never find a car parking spot as easy as I do. I will ask my guides for help in all areas of my life. I once had a conversation with my guides about promoting one of my books and at the end of the conversation we decided that I should go on TV and tell everyone about it. The very next day I received an email from a TV network asking me if I would like to come on the show and talk about relationships. The very subject of the book I was currently promoting.

I have so many examples of how using your intuitive power can help you get what you want. Everyone has this power. You can ask your guides to help you in every area of your life. Work, wealth, relationships they are there to help you, or if it sits better with you use your intuition much more.

Amazing Relationships

Having a relationship is training each other what you will or will not put up with. Patrick McNally PhD

You need to decide if your personal relationship (marriage, significant other, partner) what ever you call it is as good as it can be. Personal relationships have good times and bad, so don't be fooled into thinking the relationship must be perfect all the time. If you do then you are playing a trick on yourself. Life events get in the way as you move through your life and your partners life.

Sometimes these events are unforeseen like illness. Each time something happens unexpectedly in your life don't take it out on your partner or yourself, take a different view.

To help you understand how great relationships work I'll start by asking you to rate your current relationship out of ten.

I'd like you to rate your relationship from one being a very bad relationship right up to ten meaning your relationship is awesome. Oh and by the way you can't select five. Yes I know it might change on a daily basis, but just pick a number and write it down.

Your number is _____

Okay if your number is 7 or 8 your relationship is in a healthy place, yet could still be improved. If it is 9 or 10 then you have a very close, loving relationship. Well done keep it up. Or you may have just met and are still in the honeymoon phrase.

If your number is 4 then there are signs that you need to pay more attention to this joint relationship. If your number is 2 or 3 then you are not in a very healthy relationship and you need to take some action to resolve it now. Here is in my opinion the very best advice I can offer you. If your personal relationship isn't in order it will affect the rest of your life. So here is how to fix it.

Ask yourself what you have contributed to the relationship *that hasn't worked*. Yes you read it correct. You see people often arrive in my office with what looks like a list of items they no longer like about their spouse. Sometimes the list is three pages long. Do you think the person who made out the list is a happy person? No. However if that same person took a better look at what he or she was contributing that didn't work, instead of focusing on what the other person was doing wrong according to them, the answers would be there to see.

When you create a relationship the first thing you do is train the other person. Please get that into your mind. You train the other person every day. You let that other person know if he or she is doing right or wrong, according to your own values and opinions. Arguments begin between two people because each of them has a different view or opinion and either both or one of them cannot happily accept the other person's point of view.

When people come to see me about couple counselling (and believe me I've seen thousands of couples), they all say the same things, and I mean the same things. Isn't that alarming to you reading this? I mean you would think that at least one of the many that have spoken to me over the years would have said something I had never heard before, but no they have been all the same and as I previously outlined often accompanied with page upon page of complaints.

For example, men complain about their female spouse listing the following topics:

- o She spends too much money
- o She always complains I don't do enough
- o She is too soft with the children, not strong enough discipline
- o She wants to know where I am and what time I'm coming home

While the females complain about their men including the following topics:

- o He always complains about how much money I spend
- o He is far too angry when dealing with the children
- o He argues with me about the things I buy that he thinks I shouldn't
- o He is always moaning about a lack of money

- He doesn't communicate with me anymore

Obviously these are only a few, however I'm sure you would have encountered at least one of these in your relationship. So if every relationship suffers the same problems then how do you improve yours? It is really very easy, here's how. Every person I have ever met has told me they *compete* with their spouse and it ends up in an argument over *stupid topics*.

Of course they don't say it in those words but really that is what is going on, a competition. Look at it this way, both of you have successfully trained each other how to behave in your relationship, correct? Without you knowing, you have established a set way you both communicate. Now here is the key, you begin to compete with each other because you don't use the fundamental law of allowing. This means that if one of you had a view that is different to the other you *can't or won't accept it*.

ACCEPT – ac-cept - Come to terms with. Take something offered. Agree to. Acknowledge. Understand. Allow.

Anyway you want to look at it these are just some of many definitions of accepting. So how come we can't accept? Is it because many times you just hoped that the other person would change and then you would feel happy, so then you don't need to accept? If you take nothing else from this entire book please take this. The day you learn to accept another person's right to an opinion will be the day you have true freedom and a wonderful relationship.

Let me explain. When you learn to truly accept the rights of others it doesn't matter what they say or do, it will not affect you negatively. Look at how many times in your life you felt angry, anxious or fearful over other people's actions. Yet if you were able to accept that every person on this planet has the right to an opinion you would welcome that opinion rather than oppose it.

In a long term loving relationship both people change over their lifetime. Their opinions change, their body changes and together they both change. The change is inevitable and doesn't have to cause you stress in the relationship.

I don't expect you to agree with your spouse all the time, if you are, your relationship is in danger. I teach couples how to accept each other's point of view with mutual respect, dignity and happiness. Not scream loud abusive comments over the dinner table in front of the children just because someone doesn't agree with that point of view. Decide right now that you will become the one who accepts your partner's point of view and accepts their opinion calmly and respectfully. I mean you did in the beginning didn't you? Or was your first date full of arguments and competition?

It really is that simple, the moment you do it and not feel any emotion inside your body when your partner shares their feelings with you is the moment your relationship will improve ten fold. Once you begin to do this you will notice your partners view change, then you can ask them to do the same.

Negative People

One of the ways to live amazingly is to sack the negative people in your life, the negative energy vampires that hover around you just waiting to suck you dry. These people lead you *away* from an amazing life instead of towards it.

You know the people in your life that suddenly telephone you and when you recognise the number you take this internal sigh and think, "Oh no not you again".

Start today and go through your list of contacts and sack the people that are negative, the ones that do not enrich your life. They even do it on Facebook now. You *can* get rid of so called friends you thought you had. Use your intuition, ask yourself do you really feel as though this person gives you happiness or grief.

When you look hard enough you'll find them. Then you can begin to cultivate new and exciting people in your life. Most of the time when I ask people to do this they often tell me they feel guilty, some even say they are too afraid to end the so called friendship because the *friend* would be very angry. Can you understand that? They can't thin out their social friendships because they feel too afraid.

Tell me you know that is wrong please? This is your life, not theirs. Sort out those energy vampires and just feel happy telling them you are not into what ever they are right now and you can catch up with them some other time perhaps.

Your Significant Other

When it comes to that special person and partner in your life, you need to make certain you do the following:
- Select the right person in the first place
- Understand this person's job *isn't* to make you happy
- Be aware that the traits you see in the other person that you think are not in you, are. You just don't display them
- Be grateful for being together
- Accept that both of you will change considerably over the length of your relationship
- Know that from day one you are about to train this partner and understand that once trained if you don't like it, you need to look at you, not your partner and begin the re-training
- Accept that your priority at any time in your life is almost never going to be the other persons priority

- If you decide to breed, be sure your relationship can withstand the dramatic changes to your partnership when children arrive
- Add up before you have children just how much it will cost you to have children go to school, college, university and beyond
- By making the decision to have a family will it *stop* either of you living an amazing life

Relationships play a very important part in all our lives, so understand that your point of view is never the only one. Then also remember that if you are living with someone right now where you know you can't ever safely share your point of view without it erupting into abuse or physical violence, *get out now, fast*. You do not need to feel subservient to any other human being ever. You are unique and so is your partner. Isn't that what love is?

Please look out for my new book on relationships called, "How To Have Amazing Relationships".

How To Become An Amazing Parent

No matter what your amazing life is right now or will become later, you will encounter children. Even though you may decide not to have children yourself, I'm certain you have met children and thought to yourself, how did that happen.

I met a woman who made me smile when she told me, "Patrick I do love children, I just can't eat a whole one"

Many parents I meet have made the biggest mistake in their lives by placing more importance on the pursuit of money than on their children. Parents work long hours and children suffer. Never put money before children or your spouse, not if you want a loving relationship and an amazing life. Some people ask how the art of lovemaking can make a child that has turned out to be such a monster. Well instead of you having to go out and purchase a book on parenting, I've included how to become an amazing parent here for you.

If you are currently struggling to work out how to love and guide your children, then this chapter will give you the answers. While you are absorbing this I may smash a few myths about parenting along the way. So just read the principles and then you will understand when children become completely lost, we can rescue them.

Every day I attend my office I find myself face to face with a parent. 90% of the time it will be a mother. She will explain to me in great detail what she thinks (guesses) is wrong with her child. Then she will ask me if I would like to talk to the child to see if I can fix *it*. She then walks outside and brings the child in to sit in my office while she goes outside and waits. The expectation then of course is that the child who just walked in won't be the same child when it walks out again. Somehow I am going to *fix* this child, because obviously it's broken. Well at least that's what the mothers told me, and I have about twenty minutes to accomplish this.

So the first thing I do is remember all my training over all these years and then that little Mexican man named Cesar Millan (the dog whisperer). You can't imagine this famous television dog trainer training the dog and not the owner can you? Well in my office when it comes to training children, it involves the parents much more than the child. Just like my friend Cesar, he knows that the dog has been trained to behave in a certain way and he needs to retrain the dog owner. I need to retrain the parent as well as the child. That shouldn't be a surprise at all. Not many parents have been on training programs on how to raise a child.

In these following examples I am talking about children from the age of 8 years upwards. With the young ones ranging from 8 to 15 I can still get away with the trusted story of bank building. This is where I tell the children that no matter what they want in life, whether it's right now, at the weekend or next year, the only way the parents will say yes is if they have built enough good bankable currency to get a yes.

The Amazing Bank Technique

Children, as we would agree need both discipline and praise. By the way I use praise 90% of the time, it's easier to look for and works 100% more for the child. Most parents I meet never understand praise and what it does for the child. They are too busy looking and expecting all the wrong things to happen. Again, as I have been saying throughout this book, it is a trick of the mind, this time by the parent.

I first set up the child to understand that they need to do things around the house for free. This means jobs, any jobs they can handle. This teaches a child to contribute to the family and the household. Then once the chores are done I want the child to look for ways to build a bank of currency by way of more jobs, but this time they will use the extra jobs they do as currency.
Here's how it works:

I was asked to help a 14-year-old girl who didn't get this at all. She wanted no part of my plan at all, until I said, "I'm the only person on earth who can get your parents off your back". This got her attention. From there I explained how she would need to work very hard to reinstate herself in the family so she could be trusted by both parents again.

She had a history of running out of school, not doing homework, bad grades and bad language, all of which remember had been trained. I managed to find the missing part of this little girls puzzle by listening to her, something she told me her parents never did. She would tell me that every time she attempted to tell her parents how she felt, they simply shouted at her and told her to go to her room. So now motivated and looking forward to the next two weeks of hard work and looking for opportunities to do even more tasks for her parents, this young child left happy. I didn't say a word to the mother.

Two weeks later the mother arrived back with her daughter and began to tell me how much the child had changed. The mother went on to tell me that her daughter had begun to work around the house, was being nice to her brother and sister and staying at school. When it was the daughters turn to come in she was angry and upset. She told me she had done all I had suggested but that her parents had not said well done or anything.

This is typical of many parents who don't even know how to give praise, let alone see times when the child needs praise. I spent most time with the mother explaining my idea of her daughter building a bank of jobs and good behaviour in exchange for special treats like having a friend over to stay the night. The mother went away and began to praise her child even more. They were both very happy the last time they came in all because we retrained both of them to look at life differently.

Change What Doesn't Work

Don't allow your child to be disrespectful

Jack was an 8 year-old boy out of control (mothers description) who attended my practice for anger issues. The story was that the mother had lost control and Jack was winning and loving every minute of it. When I asked the mother if Jack misbehaved in front of his dad, the answer was no. This is a very popular situation and often can cause big trouble in the marriage or partnership. The child's view of his father is very different from the view he has of his mother.

Little Jack had his mother running scared, the mother forgot who was the adult. She spent most of her day running after him, literally. If she was trying to get him to school on time he would be too quick for her and run around the house with her chasing and yelling at him. However if dad was home little Jack was an angel. Do you get what's happening in this household? Yes, Jack is in charge and mum is not. My work had to begin with mum. I found out that mum did most of the parenting while dad was at work. However dad was fed up with mum because she couldn't control the child, so the parents were in crisis.

The simple difference here was one parent represented fear to young Jack while the other parent didn't. The dad would just have to look at the child and Jack did what he was told. Mum however had to scream, chase and often smack Jack to get him to behave. Of course like all mums do she would attempt to sit Jack down and talk to him about why he should have behaved. This technique of talking to a young child using adult language like the word respect does not work. She did this all the time and all the time it didn't work, she kept doing it.

Please remember this as long as you live your amazing life. When it comes to children and behaviour fear is a greater motivator than pain. The dad produced fear in Jack and the mother produced pain. In screaming, chasing and smacking Jack all mum produced was short-term pain that only slowed Jack down. It also trained Jack to never look for any other attention other than pain. He became used to the smacks and the screams. I always ask every parent this question. "Did you treat your parents with this much disrespect when you were that age"? The parent will almost always say, *no way.*

It still amazes me that while a mother is in the midst of telling me how disgustingly rude and disrespectful her child is she still doesn't get it. I have interrupted literally thousands of parents and asked that question. When I ask the parent why they didn't abuse their own parents they normally tell me they were *too afraid*. So of course I can't help myself and I just have to ask the obvious question.

So, why do you continue to let the little child do it then? The most common answer I hear is! "I don't know why". The real answer is they became afraid themselves as parents. That's why they teach bad manners to their children. The parents become so afraid that in their mind it would be easier to let the child misbehave than have to tackle it head on. A child needs your love yes, but you need to train that child. The problem is it's the other way around. Let me explain.

An Out of Control Teenager

I had two parents of a wild 15 year-old girl arrive at my office in tears. Monica by the parents account was without a doubt totally in control of both parents. She had obviously had similar training at an early age just like young Jack. Both parents had run out of ideas. Here is what they told me they had done so far to change the girl's behaviour.

- o Taken away her mobile phone (why does a 15 year-old child need a mobile phone I hear you say to yourself?)
- o Grounded her, which means not going out other than school

- Stopped her from going on the computer and internet

So that was it, that was all they had done and they sat in my office, the mother with tears rolling down her cheeks and the father the same. I had them understand that they were sat in my office with the weight of the world on their shoulders and their daughter was running their lives and loving it. I didn't even have to see the child. It was the parents that needed more help, so here is what I told them to do. Now I already knew how they would react to what I was about to suggest in the way of new strategies, but I also knew that from years of doing it this way, it would give us the correct outcome.

I began by telling them that her bedroom door needed to be removed and all of her clothes had to go. Then any trinkets, other furniture and makeup, all had to go. They were to empty the child's room until all that was left was a mattress on the floor and her school uniform. They had to make sure all the rest was taken to another place. While I was outlining this strategy the two parents were looking even more afraid than when they walked in. Then I told them to telephone all of their daughter's friend's parents and let them know that under no circumstances were they to allow their daughter in to their house if she was to run away again.

As I continued with my plan the mother couldn't cope any longer and had to interrupt. I was waiting for her. Imagine this, here is me jumping out of my chair and writing on the big whiteboard all the things we were going to do to their precious little baby!!! The mother didn't disappoint me. Just like others before her she made attempts to let me know why they couldn't do what I was asking them to do. Even the father jumped in and said he thought the whole door thing was a little tough. Now this happens every day in my office so you will have to forgive me for sounding a little tough here, but this always delivers the state of mind in the parents I need to help them further.

    I began to scream and shout at the top of my lungs at both of them. How dare you both tell me what you can and cannot do, what sort of parents are you anyway? Are you bad parents then, is that is? Do you hit her all the time? Do you give up on her because you can't get past your own feelings? Is that it? Are you hiding behind your own poor me attitude? As I continued my rant I was in fact helping them get into a state of extreme fear and panic. Remember humans make up thoughts and emotions that produce behaviour. These parents with the help of Monica had created an entire state of chaos and through perceived fear couldn't parent the child. Both parents began to defend and make excuses saying I was taking it too far and that the punishment didn't fit the crime. I was even more incensed than before. Now they were telling me that Monica, a 15 year-old girl who swears and abuses her family and drinks and smokes and stays out all night doesn't deserve any punishment. I hadn't even called it punishment, they did and the reason they called it punishment was because they couldn't bring themselves to do anything about it.

Now that the three of us were in the middle of a heated debate and both parents were in a state of fear and dread I wanted to make sure they knew I was serious about sorting this mess out. So I finished off by telling them that if they didn't do as they were told I'd make sure the authorities found out from my report that they were both terrible parents. The reaction was the same as all the rest, they stopped, looked pale and their breathing became intense, just like a panic attack. Now was the moment that would change their lives forever.

Unknown to them during our little heated debate the mother kept putting her left arm onto her chest and breathing shallow every time I suggested things she should be doing. The father was similar as his tummy was busy moving in and out at the thought of removing his daughter's bedroom door. So I had the mother sit in my big black *magic chair*. I call it magic because that's where the magic of change often happens. I had her tell me where she felt the dread and fear inside her and as expected it was in her chest. I had her close her eyes and see the image that helped her become afraid. Then I had her shrink that image smaller and smaller until it was the size of a *postage stamp* and then blow it away. As she was doing that I had her rub her chest side ways across with her hand.

When she opened her eyes the fear had gone completely. I then did the same with the father and his result was the same, his fear had gone. Now I had two parents with no fear at all. I have to do the same technique with every parent that brings in a child that has become out of control. This I might add was the start of their change of view. With two parents who were not afraid anymore the task at hand became more manageable. They both listened to all the careful instructions and plans I had laid out for them both to do and they were to come back a week later. Now you can see why I needed to have these parents truly feel and experience the pain they were going through at that moment. I cannot cure a phobia of spiders unless I have a spider to use to make sure the person really feels the emotion, even though you now know we make all these fears up by ourselves. I can't help someone overcome a fear of heights unless they make an attempt to be up high with me.

These parents began their conversation believing that Monica, at 15 years of age was out of control and they didn't know how to stop it. It all became very painful emotionally and overcome with these made up emotions the parents couldn't cope. Now they could understand their contribution to what didn't work before. By having the parents reach a height of panic and anxiety that was as real as they could feel, it had a much more powerful affect when the fear was removed so quickly. I was then able to dismantle that feeling in a heartbeat.

It is so rewarding to see parents after this first session, which I fondly call "Imposing Sanctions". I have my brother in-law Keith to thank for that one by the way. This particular couple were even more joy to work with because they truly loved not only their daughter, but also each other. Sometimes I'm faced with a couple that have lost the love they once had for each other, so then they communicate differently with the children which can cause all sorts of problems. If a couple is not together on this it is very difficult to accomplish a complete turn around of bad behaviour by parents and children alike.

When they arrived back they had smiles on their faces, which is always a good sign for me. They told me the child had reacted exactly as I had predicted. She had screamed loudly, thrown things around the house and ran away to her best friends place. However the best friends mum had done as Monica's parents asked and not allowed her to stay in their home. Once again I see these techniques bring success to parents.

There is almost always one person, normally a female (sorry no disrespect meant) who for personal reasons feels the need to become Mother Teresa the second. You know the one I mean. She is normally a single mother (nothing wrong with them by the way) who is in desperate need of love and attention herself. She will be the one who no matter what a parent might tell her, knows best and will no matter what you tell her *still take your child in for the night.* She gets off on it. She craves this feeling she gets when a child runs away from home only to find refuge in her house. It is real and there are women who believe they should do this.

I had warned this couple that if they had one of these in their community then their daughter would know who she was and go there. Sure enough their daughter knew about this woman and tried to enter but this couple had taken notes and remembered. Cleverly the parents had asked a close friend to go and see this woman that night, so you can imagine the feeling this 15 year-old girl had when she had exhausted all other places to go, only to discover her mothers best friend was there and demanded she leave at once. This woman was also able to explain to Mother Teresa the second that everything was going according to plan and there was no need for her to worry. Poor dear!!

The couple attended to every detail, they locked up their home like a fortress, turned off all the lights and went to bed. Sure they sat there worried, but they had each other to talk to and reassure that what they were doing was for the good of their child.

Now please remember this was a kid who knew her way around the streets, she was no angel of innocence. For the past two years she had broken away, put fear into her parents and walked the streets. However I was changing her little game. I had done this with hundreds of parents and when the parents carried out the plan to the letter it always worked. Always.

They told me just on 1.30am in the early morning they heard a knock on the back door and it was her. They remembered what to do. Both parents went to the door and didn't open it, but asked who was there. The daughter answered and the parent's job was to listen to her voice and make sure they heard something other than anger. I didn't want them to see her, just listen to her voice first. The daughter was weeping, she had walked everywhere she could to seek shelter and friends but found no one. It was in the middle of winter and the child had run out in a fit of anger and didn't take any warm clothing. Well her parents got rid of everything remember!

How different was that to the times she had ran away and gloated to her friends about how she could do what she wanted to? The parents said they were convinced that their daughter was genuine in her tears and upon that they went about their next part. I use the house door as a symbol, I wanted the child to really understand and feel what it was like to have no where to go and that if she was smart she would return home a different child.

Before opening the door the parents outlined what her life would be like this time around. They had their list of requests and *must haves* in order to let her back into the house and back into the family. If she agreed to these then they would open the door and they would all start with a clean sheet, no nagging and bringing up old issues.

If she didn't agree then they would turn the light off and go back to sleep, leaving her on her own.

No wonder they were smiling, I was by then, they had been brilliant. However to my surprise the father moved to the door of my office and opened it and in walked this 15 year-old daughter of theirs. I was totally surprised and wondering if I was about to get yelled at from her when she walked over and gave me a hug and said, "Mum and Dad told me you put our family back together for us, thank you so much". Well I can honestly tell you there wasn't a dry eye in the office after that, even the parents hadn't thought she would say that.

This family in crisis felt the same emotional pain millions of other families do across our planet. My hope in telling you about this family is to let you know there is such a thing as a happy family and if your family is in crisis the number one thing to remember is, don't trick your mind into thinking the child will do terrible things if you don't let them have what they want. Children have to grow, they have to test and understand emotions. I've heard just about all the threats a child can offer to a parent and to me. The child can and does attempt to convince their parents that these idle threats will be carried out. Once you give in to these *so-called* threats, you have just trained that child to use them against you.

Remember You're the Parent

If for any reason you are dealing with your child and you suddenly feel anxious or fearful, instantly remove your negative feelings before you continue the conversation. If you don't you will believe the child will harm itself and then *you* will become a parent afraid to discipline the child or give it a wonderful loving childhood, because you are coming from a view of fear and what if. Don't get fooled by threats of a child, these threats are really cries for help and they need their parents to take massive action to change things.

For example, an 11 to 16 year old wants to know if they fit in with others. This becomes their primary important priority in their life at this age. So communicate with them on this topic often so you can reassure them that they do in fact fit in. Remember once children go to school

YOU ARE NO LONGER THE MOST IMPORTANT PERSON IN THEIR LIFE ANYMORE... so get over it and enjoy your life

I realise that this may come as a shock to some parents but please understand. Your love as a parent has to be a love of allowing, allowing them to fall, so they may get back up, a love of allowing them to fail, so they alone can work out how to succeed. Only then have you prepared your child for adulthood effectively. All parents want so much more for their children and sometimes that love can blind them. Parents often use the phrase, "I just want to give my children what I never had". In saying this though I believe we should be teaching them how to be happy for no reason rather than attempting to run a comparison on how our own childhood was. It should have no meaning to your own child's life, but we know it does. The best way to teach your children to live an amazing life is to live one yourself. Teach by doing not by saying.

If you over compensate in order to rid yourself of the guilt and shame you still feel because of your own childhood, your child will suffer. Over protective parents can ruin a young life before it has a chance to blossom. Love your children but give them the freedom to learn from their actions and to take responsibility for their actions.

I used to read to my four sons when they were young and when I could I would always bring in a new book but make up the story rather than read the book. As my sons grew up I would tell them stories about what it was like when their great, great grandfather was alive, then about my life as a young boy their age.

They heard stories about how people would have to stand in a line all day in the pouring rain just to buy sugar. Times like that in our planets evolution that should teach lessons to future generations. Today my sons are fathers and they often mention that those stories really grounded them and made them feel grateful and appreciate what they had and to understand what others didn't have. My sons today as fathers battle the minefields of mobile phones, internet and social network websites with their own children. I remind them to let their children know that once we could all walk down the high street shopping and if anyone was thirsty we would stop at one of the many drink fountains scattered along the street for a drink of *FREE* water. Today they build massive complexes and round you up in concrete shopping malls where the only place you can get water is out of a plastic bottle that costs you a fortune.

Here's the real issue. As the world continues to change so too should your skills as a parent.

Amazing Love Of A Child

Today it's the parents who *need* the love of the child because the parent isn't living an amazing life. Many of the parents I see have shattered relationships and marriages and highly stressful lives. So in order to have love the parent craves for the love of their child at any cost. Then when it's time to say no to the child and mean no the parent can't. Now we have a guilty parent and an out of control child being trained by the unwitting parent.

I can't remember how many smart little children have sat in my office and told me how useless their parents are.

They tell me things like "Patrick, my parents take my iPod from me for being naughty. They say it's gone for a week, but I know I'll have it back in two days, Mum always gives in".

This is the type of parenting that confuses a child and trains them that the parent doesn't mean what is said and therefore they can do anything they want.

Parents live in fear of many things today. You don't need to believe that trick. Stop, don't buy the myth of the child's threat. Instead be that honest reliable parent. This rubbish and politically correct phrase that the child has rights has been well over used.

No one has ever stopped me from filming or taking pictures of my children or grandchildren. Plenty have tried but I told them to go away or else. They got the message.

YOU ARE SUPPOSED TO BE PARENTS NOT A FRIEND TO YOUR CHILDREN

Today in some supposedly civilised communities a 12 year-old child has been given the lawful right to choose which parent to live with in the case of parents separating and at that same age they can even divorce their parents. Can you really believe this stupidity? What was the name of that dumb person who was stupid enough to come up with that legislation and when did other humans on this planet suddenly become righteous enough to tell others what they can and can't do as a parent?

My advice is simple, tell the *do gooders* of the world to *mind their own business*. You are the parent and its your birthright to love, cherish and bring up your children anyway you want. Otherwise it will be these small fanatically stupid and supposedly *politically correct idiots* that will tell you that we all have to bow to their view of their world. Don't believe their trick. They would have you believe that behind every grandparent taking a video of his grandchildren's Christmas pageant lays a pedophile.

The media has conned you out of all pure happiness and reason when it comes to parenting, just look at what they dish you up as news. Do you really need to hear all the bad stories about parents and children? Does bad news about a child suddenly alert you to harm, or make you feel happy? No of course not, but you get my point don't you? Filter your world of made up media news and you can concentrate on the lives of you and your family.

Your role is to love your child and teach right from wrong and how to have good manners. You can only do that by making sure you yourself live an amazing life first. What about all the wonderful people that have impacted our lives already with their amazing life. Do you think their parents were told they couldn't do this or that for the child? No.

Tiger Woods was raised by a father who loved playing golf, was the father wrong? Did he get told that it was not acceptable and if he did, did he agree with them? No. Greg Norman had a mother who played golf and the list is endless of people worldwide who have lived amazing lives, because their parents played a pivotal role in their lives. The parents in this example had a right to show their children what life could be like if they chose golf as their life.

In cities and towns all over the world parents and children make up that society in any way they choose, so don't be fooled by people telling you that you cannot do this or that with your children. In England there isn't a father who wouldn't want his son to play soccer or rugby for his favourite club or country. They are your own children and you have a right to provide a safe, loving childhood for them and help them design their life journey.

I am not denying that the other side of the coin is where we hear bad stories about child abuse. However we wouldn't have as much child abuse if we had adults living a free and happy amazing life would we? Children are wonderful at following their parents, why wouldn't they. The parent is after all the most significant person in the young child's life.

So there you have it, how to be an amazing parent. Live your own amazing life so your children feel it and experience it through your actions. Not your words. Put on a new pair of glasses and rediscover how much praise you can give your child, then when the behaviour of the child needs correcting, you can issue punishment that *fits the crime.*

Teach them good manners. Keep onto them all the time, remind them to say thank you and please or excuse me. These are vital to a child's self esteem. If they have great manners they will sense the warm friendly responses of others they communicate with. Be consistent. Always keep your word, no matter what. So take a moment before you rush into saying something to your children that you may later regret.

Explain when giving punishment or imposing sanctions why you are doing it. Do not get into a discussion about it, just tell them why and make sure the child *never* has the last word. The teaching point here is for your children to *accept* the punishment, know why it is in place and learn not to repeat the behaviour again. No matter how bad it gets, no matter how bad you think you feel about what is happening in you and your children's worlds right now, remember this. It's not about your own personal feelings of anxiety, guilt, shame or even pride as a parent, it's about teaching your loved ones how to be ready to live an amazing life.

Enjoy the journey together and know that the ups and downs will arrive as sure as the sun and rain. Know some times will be more challenging than others and enjoy looking at both perspectives as you and your child learn together.

It's what you do as a parent that defines your child's perception of life, not what you say

Wealth

I haven't met one person yet that doesn't want more wealth. Therefore I'm making the assumption that you also could do with some extra cash. So if we look at some statistics we will discover there are predominately two schools of thought when it comes to wealth. One view is that 99% of the world population doesn't have enough money. This leaves a very small percentage with loads and loads of wealth. As a young man I was often baffled by those figures. Why is it that only 1% have all the wealth? I mean after all there is plenty of money circulating in the world isn't there? The other view is 97% of the world's population don't have wealth and 3% have it.

Whichever way you wish to look at it, the alarming thing is, why so few? Is there a secret? Do the few who have it keep it under lock and key? Is it something they say, do or feel? I soon found out that there are two types of people when it comes to wealth. The Consumer and The Breeder. The breeders of course are the wealthy. The consumers simply spend their money and most of the time spend way over what they even earn. If you think about it this makes it almost (if not totally) impossible to build wealth.

However, if you look past the figures into why this happens you will discover 99% of the population do not have building wealth high on their priority. In fact they would list things like a new TV set higher than building wealth. Why? Well I've heard many reasons. Some people tell me they want more money but they are impatient and just can't stick to a plan or a budget. That at least is accurate. They will never be wealthy with that strategy in place.

As my private client list reads like a who's who of the rich and famous, and not so famous I should add, I thought I'd begin a little research of my own. So every time the emails and text messages came in and it was one of my celebrity clients, I'd fly to wherever they were in the world, fix them and then ask as many questions as I could about how they built wealth. With no exception everyone over the period I researched said the same. They all agreed that they had great wealth because to them they never had to go to work for a living. Every single one of them told me what they did for a living didn't feel like a job because they all loved what they did.

What if Joe DiMaggio or Babe Ruth had placed becoming an American Baseball legend on their list of priorities at number 30. Do you think they would have had the same results? No I don't think they would have, you see you never had to ask either of them to go hit a ball. They were totally motivated from within to play baseball every day as long as they could. No one had to ask them to practice, it became their magnificent obsession.

They like others who excel in their chosen profession never ever needed outside motivation. Now you know why their values are in order. They know that if they want to be the best actor, sportsman, business leader, mother or father then their values and priorities need to match that goal.

It's fun at my workshops when I ask people to write down their top 20 priorities. I ask them at the beginning of the event so they can see how their values and priorities affect their own lives. So by the time we have finished the program they understand that it's impossible to achieve anything in their life unless it's a high priority and it fits within their own value system.

Now if we already know we can trick our own mind then why don't we look at how we can deliberately trick our mind, but this time, trick it into believing we can attain great wealth. Just like the Phobic who manufactures false fear and sends the chemicals down to their body, we can do the same. We can trick our mind into believing anything. Do you know the old saying *fake it till you make it*? Well that's what a lot of people have been shown. The world was swamped with self-help books that told us all we had to do was fake it till we made it and everything would work.

The only thing wrong with that was they never actually told you how to do it. They just said *do it*. Today modern day television self-help gurus tell us to meditate or do affirmations every day. Come on please, do you really think people stand in front of their mirror every day and say "I'm a wealthy person" when they are behind in their mortgage and can't pay their bills?

Besides, this technique only uses your 7% conscious mind so it is often difficult for people to sustain. The idea of saying nice happy thoughts to yourself is a great idea in theory but how do you remember to do it? What if you forget one day because you had a bad sleep or something happened that upset you in the morning? Maybe the kids are running late for the school bus, then what? Can you imagine a busy Mum running late for school racing to the bathroom in an angry state shouting, "I'm bloody happy and money will flow to me, now get in the car kids quick ".

Remembering to do your affirmations is very hard for most people to incorporate into their lives because it's all conscious mind work. That means that you are trying to trick your mind into thinking you are wealthy with only 7 % of your total mind.

A Blueprint For Building Wealth

This exercise will help you understand just how important wealth truly is. Many people say they want wealth but end up with very little. Here is how you will discover *if you will ever* have great wealth.
- List your top 20 values (what is most important to you) from 1 down to 20, the first being the

most important thing in your life right now. What they are now today, be honest.
- After that wherever you listed wealth, unless it's number three or four move it up there now and then list 50 benefits for you moving wealth to within your top five. If you want to build wealth it must be in the top five. You see if you don't list enough benefits you will never have the words to tell yourself it's real, then wealth will never arrive in your life and you'll be a 99% consumer, instead of a wealthy 1%er!!!!

When you have listed all the benefits of moving wealth higher in your priorities you need to read them and discover how you feel about the changes. Some people become very excited about it, while others feel anxious. How will you feel? Do the exercise and find out. When the *why* is big enough the *how to* takes care of itself. By this I mean if the reasons you have listed are real enough and big enough you will discover that your mind will work out how this will happen.

Earlier I mentioned that many people I have met didn't know what type of life they wanted, they said their life just happened. Now this is your moment to design your new life, rather than just let it happen. There is nothing worse than waking up one day and realising your life has passed you by and you then think it's too late to change it.

Remember everyone is a millionaire you just may not have cashed yours in yet

The exciting part of my job is to watch as my clients begin to change their life, it's truly amazing. Now your turn has arrived and I'm grateful to you for letting me show you how. For all the years you have been living your mind has been storing a bank of wealth for you. Only you and the way you operate in the world have this special unique wealth. I call it your life experience. Your knowledge is specific only to you and your experience is your wealth sat inside of you right now. The only thing you haven't done yet is turned that abundance into specific wealth.

You see it's because we are all so unique that amazing lives can be created. The most difficult thing people tell me they have to do is make a decision on this. Just make a decision. That decision by the way is how you will display your wealth to yourself first. Remember Mother Teresa displayed her wealth by helping dying souls in their hour of need. Bill Gates displayed his wealth by helping people use computer software. They both served the greater world and they both went outside their world and provided service to others. That is true wealth and if you want abundant wealth then you *must* understand that we are all serving each other *first*.

Most people think of wealth in terms of cash. That's okay, however it's no good sitting there meditating about attracting money into your life if you don't go to work. In my Amazing Wealth Creation Seminar I had a person approach me before the seminar began and tell me he had been trying to attract money to him through the use of powerful meditation and the buzz words of his day, The Law Of Attraction. When I asked him how much he was worth he said it hadn't worked at all and that he was now very depressed. I then found out he and his family were all on unemployment payments every fortnight.

How can a person sit at home and wish for money for the sake of money. To make matters worse, here was a family who had never worked in a decade. He hadn't nor had his father. Yet they had all the TV sets and other consumer items everyone who does work had. Obviously this guy had played a trick of the mind on himself, just like his father before him. It ended cool though, this guy went away and found a job within a week to the surprise of his entire family.

Now you can see how powerful playing a trick on yourself can be. If you are ready and want to exchange your inner wealth experience for cash or for a new career or even for a cause far greater than yourself, all you have to do is use your mind, feel totally soulfully grateful and the world will notice you. When you find a passion or a cause that is far greater than your own mortal self no obstacle on planet earth will ever stop you from attaining that. Remember the grandmother and her quest for a safer rail system?

Let's say you have decided to use your inner wealth and knowledge and to have more money come to you. Here is how you would do it. First you would list 150 reasons why you are grateful for the life you have right at this moment. After all, so far you have been the one who has created it. Yes, today right now as you read this sentence, list 150 reasons why you are grateful. Remember that the reason we are listing these on paper is to give yourself the motivation and reason to change your behaviour easily and happily. You need to start from a place of gratitude so you can create the building blocks to wealth. How many times have you read about someone gaining wealth only to later lose it all. At first they focused on *wanting* wealth and then once they had wealth they became worried and then focused on not *losing* it.

You can't be grateful and worried about losing money at the same time

You do not have great monetary wealth it is because it wasn't high enough on your list of priorities. Now is the time to change that. It's time to get real about your life right now.

Don't read anymore until you have your list complete

Now you have 150 reasons why you are grateful, make sure you read these as often as you can during the next few hours while we do this. Whenever you feel any negative emotion arriving in your mind or body, go to this list and remind yourself how grateful you are, the power of change lies within this list.

You need to make another decision. This one is simple. Will you work for someone or will you work for yourself in a business you own? When you have made that choice we can move on. So write it down here in the book *now*!!!.

_____

As you begin to think about this question of your own business or not, make sure you listen to your intuition and your body. Remember that your body will play tricks on you if you are not listening. Notice when you think about this decision how it makes you feel.

When you think of working for another person, say a local business in your town or city, do you become excited or fearful? When you think of owning your own business do you also feel the emotions pouring into your body?

Either way you pose this question of yourself when your body responds, you have just tricked your mind there and then. Inside every human there is a longing for freedom. The freedom to do whatever they want with their lives. You also have an inner longing to make an impact on the world, it maybe that you haven't been able to shed the fear enough for you to accept wealth yet. Your list will kick start your journey to wealth and financial freedom. Use it, refine it and add to it all the time.

Money

Have you ever wondered why some people are living on the street, while others live in luxury? Have you ever thought to yourself, what choices did that particular person make? What happened in their lifetime that resulted in one person living in poverty on the street and the other in luxury? Six out of ten couples I see tell me that they blame a lack of money as a major reason for their relationship problems. So when you think about it, the subject of money enters everyone's life sooner or later. There isn't a topic that creates more passion than money. When people share their beliefs about money you can understand why there have been so many books written about it.

How many books on the subject of money have you purchased? How many have you read? More importantly, when was the last book you read about *How To Not Have Money* or better still a book on *Here's How To Lose All Your Money And End Up Broke*. In our capitalist society we write books on money and great wealth and put immense value on money. Money in many peoples minds is a way to separate the have and the have not's. Imagine reading a book about how to have no money. It would start off by showing you how to live well above your means and spend much more than you earn. I see many people in my practice everyday do it that way. They must have read this book. Then the book would show you how to not run a budget, so you can buy anything when you like for no particular reason, have you seen that happen before?

So where and how did everyone learn to use up more money than they have? Obviously money is a major focus in many people's lives, yet so many people take one step forward and four back when it comes to money. Some people give up everything for the sake of money, they push themselves and others for one reason only, the pursuit of money. They give up time with a family just to make that extra dollar. Then they go and undo it all by not working to a budget and not understanding tax laws or basic financial management.

However, it's more than just accruing knowledge about money, it's the beliefs you have about it. Couples I see argue over money all the time. He says he works every hour possible for money only to find they still don't have enough to go around. She on the other hand doesn't value money the same way as he does. Her values are completely different.

As a child you may have had parents who gave you pocket money or a weekly allowance. Whatever you called it, some children received it and some children didn't. For the children that did receive money, some had to do jobs around the house and be seen to earn their money, while other children received their money because their parents believed they should receive it. Then for the children who didn't receive money they didn't really know what it was like to have money, so some of them didn't really care. While other children who didn't receive money, but knew children who did, were affected in other ways.

Living in an Irish household, sometimes our parents didn't have enough money to go around, let alone hand out extra to nine children. Can you imagine us all lining up with our hands out waiting for a penny? It was far more important to arrive at the dinner table early so you might be able to pinch a potato off the plate without being caught. So, like my family and probably your family, we all had, and still have, different values when it comes to the subject of money.

You learned about money the same way you learned other things in your life, you observed, and then experienced it. I was asked to work with a Stock Broking company once to find out how these people enjoy investing other people's money and still be able to sleep at night, but became really stressed when they gambled their own money. It wasn't rocket science to discover that it was really easy to spend other people's money, but when it came to their own they would change their state completely, which was what their problem was. As soon as they were able to enjoy spending their own money the same way they did with other people's money, the brokers earned more money and enjoyed their jobs more.

How many times can you remember someone in your family giving you money? Did you have uncles and aunties or big sisters and brothers who gave you money? Did you ever hear them say now put that away for a rainy day? Well, if you lived in Ireland, it bloody rains every day, so we would go off and spend it the same day we received it. The value of money is a direct distinction you have with your life. Some people do not value money at all. They are very happy living in a house that doesn't belong to them. They pay their rent and enjoy life through the eyes of their family and friends. These people are normally very content with life and happily do a job, any job and go home to peace and loved ones.

Then of course you can have people who are obsessed with money. I was asked to work with some board members of an international company some years ago. They were attempting to pull off a take over, which sounded hostile, but were not reaching agreement between themselves. My role as Facilitator was to find out what was stopping this and fix it. I get all the easy jobs. As my taxi pulled into their underground car park, the first thing I noticed was the standard of cars. This wasn't your average car park. Rolls Royce, Ferraris, Lamborghinis,

Bentleys. It was a who's who of the up market car industry.

Each parking space had a name attached to it and was gold plated. It would appear that these people enjoyed the spoils of their labour, or spending shareholders money, and it looked as though there was plenty of competition in the car stakes. As I got to know some of these people more throughout the weekend conference, they were lamenting their troubles even to the point where one person mentioned that their yacht was bigger than the chairman's yacht. I'm not sure why he bothered to tell me this, but it certainly helped me later with my negotiations.

Even at the highest level of wealth, money ruled, yet it was what money meant to each of these board members that mattered most. What does money mean to you? Do you live your life for the pursuit of money? Do you envy people who have lots of money? What amount of money would you be happy with in your bank account today? More importantly, what does money really provide you with? I heard a person describe money as the exchange of paper (now plastic) with pictures of dead people on them. You need to exchange something and that is normally your time for these bits of paper and then you go and exchange those bits of paper for other things, like a car, house or food.

So money to them is nothing more than a trading tool. You trade it for those things you want and then go back and trade some more of your time and then repeat the process. It amazes me when I conduct my Small Business Seminars how many business owners don't even pay themselves first. When we talk about money these small business owners always say they don't have enough to go around, so they don't get paid. I ask them if they have ever heard of a company director going without their pay packet in a large international corporation. All you have to do is read the national papers anywhere in the world and you can see evidence of mass hysteria and greed when it comes to money and directors cheating shareholders out of millions.

Yet even though these small business operators come to the seminar to learn, with many of them wanting to turn their small business into a large business, the beliefs they hold about money are stopping them growing the company. They pay bills and pay everyone else except themselves. How dumb is that? They trade their life to their dream in business and don't get paid, and then wonder why they feel tired, jaded and unmotivated.

There are experts that tell us that the more money you earn, the more you spend. Somehow your expenses go up in line with your increased earnings. That doesn't seem to figure though when you look at the amount of credit card debt these days. The people who I am talking about here are the people who do not have control of their increasing debt on their credit card. These people earn a set amount each year, but spend thousands of dollars more than that by using credit. Living far in excess of their means is one way to cause family stress and discomfort. Yet these people live their life chasing debt and not knowing what it feels like to have money of their own. Then if something happens and they are unemployed for a while, their house is gone.

If you want to understand what money can and will do for you in your life I suggest you do the following:

- First start by creating a good state of mind for yourself. Make sure you feel really powerful. This state can be made simply by closing your eyes and re-living a time when you felt this inner powerful state
- Secondly, while you are in this powerful state, create a life for yourself and your family where you have more than enough money for the rest of your life. See in your mind's eye yourself living in a place where you want to live. See yourself driving a car you want to drive. See yourself wearing the clothes you want to wear. As well as seeing yourself, you need to hear yourself, and feel how good it is to have things in abundance. These are your things
- Then check and see if the last exercise made you truly feel good, or was there interference? Did you ask questions of yourself? Did you talk to yourself and say things like, this is a waste of time or this won't work? If you did have voices or images that got in the way, it might

mean that your true values about money are mixed

Here's what I mean. You may long for more money, or think that money would solve your problems, but it won't. Deep down you may resent what money can do for you, that's incongruence and that means you are not in agreement with yourself. It could be that you say money means nothing to you at all, but deep down you crave it. Or it could be that you are worried that if you did ever have wealth you wouldn't know what to do with it, so again you have mixed feelings about money. It might be that you have a really stupid belief that you don't deserve money. With that belief, you certainly won't be attracting any wealth into your life.

Until you are able to make a clear image in your mind of what it is you truly desire and have that image make you feel really good, then you and money are going to be in conflict. List your beliefs on money. Do you think money is good or bad? What does it mean to you in your life? By simply writing it down allows your mind to direct you. Remember your mind is designed to prevent pain and seek pleasure, it's up to you what you think money represents to you.

Can You Own Your Own Business?

I have a seminar called "How To Start An Amazing Business". It's designed for people who are thinking about starting a business and also help business owners to increase their company wealth. A woman came up to me during one of the breaks in this workshop and asked if I thought she could start her own business and be successful. I hear this type of question all the time. Well what do you think my answer was? I said of course you can, yes. Anyone can start a business. As I spoke to her explaining it, I noticed she went white in the face and almost passed out. She was playing a trick of the mind on herself. She didn't know I knew of course. So I thought I should move her out of that delusion, as it wasn't real and besides it doesn't look cool in your own seminar when an audience member passes out.

I asked her what her hobbies were. She said she loved to travel and went away as often as she could. I kept *digging* because in my occupation I teach Life Coaches the art of drilling down by asking quality questions and I was doing just that. The more I asked her questions about how travel made her feel, the more she moved her mind and body into a wonderful excited and passionate state. Then I did the opposite, I mentioned things like long waits in airports and bad service and anything else I could think of. She just defended everything I made comment of. The long waits in airports she thought was wonderful, it gave her time to check out all the brochures on places she hadn't been before.

Without her knowing I was helping her make a list of all the benefits of travel in her world, then attempting to make another list of negatives about it, however there wasn't anything on that list. So here is a woman who again had tricked her mind into believing she loved travel and no matter what happened she was excited to be travelling. It had obviously become a very high priority for her. One week after the seminar she sent me an email saying she had taken my advise about becoming a travel writer and booked into a college to study. To my delight and surprise I received another email from her two years later telling me she was now a travel writer travelling the world commenting on places. All I said to her was, "Go from my seminar today and write a list of 150 benefits for strangers who have never heard of you, why they should travel to a place you have just discovered for them. List another 150 reasons why they would be grateful for your insight and honesty about these places all over the world."

To her credit she did just that and today lives her amazing life. Travel had been the priority, yet she hadn't realised that she could do what she loves and get rewarded for it. She went from freelance writing to owning her own publishing company. This was a person who like many others had first thought they couldn't do it. So even though we could argue that this woman had an un-balanced perspective on travel we made it work totally in her favour and she went onto an amazing life. However not all tricks of the mind in business work out so good.

Bankruptcy

In my opinion the single biggest fear that stops budding entrepreneurs is Bankruptcy. This dread manifests itself in a person and if left unchecked can totally destroy them and their business. Now you may not be aware that many wealthy people have failed much bigger and more times than you have. Just take a look at this very short list of people you may have heard of that were once bankrupt.

Walt Disney and Henry Ford went bankrupt. Did you know that the 16th President of the United States, Abraham Lincoln filed for bankruptcy twice? Bjorn Borg the brilliant German tennis star. Singer Natalie Cole also lost the lot. Even the founder of General Motors, William C Durant went bankrupt. Another founder, this time of Heinz Ketchup lost it all. You didn't know TV Host Larry King was bankrupt back in the late 70's did you? Finally authors Mark Twain and Oscar Wilde and none other than Donald Trump, who today is doing okay for himself.

These amazing people dared to live an amazing life. Sure you can comment on their lives and find fault somewhere, however the point is they went for it. They made a decision and had a go and even after the trauma of being bankrupt they still had that burning passion and obviously it was their number one priority. If you understand anything else here know that we all would have stopped and ran away if it was us trying to do what these legends did. It was *their priority* that kept them going. Their vision was bigger than the problem of bankruptcy, they could keep going despite that hurdle.

You will find times I'm sure where you may feel fearful or anxious about taking risks with money and business. However unless your mission is much bigger than you, you will fail. It has to be big otherwise it won't keep you moving through all the obstacles that stop others. You have to think big and serve others on a vast scale to be wealthy. You have to love what you do and do what you love to truly feel wealthy both inside your soul and in your bank balance.

When you sit in your home all supposedly safe and secure think of these people for a moment. They walked away from the very thing that keeps you from being a multi-millionaire today. They left their security and went out into the world to create a legacy, to live an amazing life. Each of them in their own way served others with what they brought to the world, yet do you sit at home afraid to even have a go? If you do then think about this for a moment. Henry Ford didn't invent the car, what he did do was work out a way to mass produce cars at affordable prices, but he lost his money before he realised his dream first time around. However just take a look at what life was like back then. It was 1908 when the Model T Ford car was first sold to the public. Back then there were no roads for a car to drive on. There wasn't any need for a car because people all lived close to where they worked. They worked long hours so didn't have time for anything else.

Horse and carts, donkeys and bikes were the way to travel. There were no petrol stations to fill up your car, so how on earth did a man decide to take such a risk and change the face of the planet? It was number one on his priority list, that's how he did it! Of course now we look back and understand that once cars became popular other related industries came on board. People got into the gasoline business and before long service stations were popping up all over the country.

Bankruptcy didn't hold Henry Ford back because making a car for the masses was his number one priority. No matter whether he went bankrupt or not, his passion took him past the every day details of a mere bankruptcy proceeding. His *immortal vision* was bigger than any obstacles the world could throw in his face. So the importance he placed on his goal met with his values perfectly, that is why you can copy Henry Ford or any other legend. The fear of losing money never stopped him and it shouldn't ever stop you. If your dream is big enough, if your number one priority is to build a business then that is what you should be doing. Not with fear or anxiety, but build it with passion and excitement and always end your day feeling grateful.

Celebrities

I was in the Australian city of Brisbane conducting a seminar, and a lady kept coming up at the breaks to ask questions. This in itself isn't strange but it was the questions this lady kept asking. Questions like, do you work with people who are in the public eye? Well, I believe everyone is in the public eye, other than those people who choose to stay indoors all day. This lady kept asking questions like, so if you did help a person like a public figure, would you ever tell anyone who it was or what is was for? As I had already told her previously I am not at liberty to break client confidentiality. It would be up to the client, but these days I have my own confidentially agreement so they also can't say anything.

I don't feel the need to have wacky celebrities running around talking to every magazine about how they were finally healed or some other rubbish. Celebrities like that are often known to use the media to their own ends and then I'd find myself being asked dumb questions from the media about what was wrong and how I fixed it. So it was little surprise that as I was leaving the stage she was the first one to appear. She asked if I could speak to her and I explained that normally after an event like this it's at least an hour before I am finished and then I have to catch a flight. She stood her ground and changed her language and she said, "I must see you before you fly out, it's critical". Well, the word critical got me, I thought wow what could be so important that it's critical? So I said I'd give her five minutes as I waited for a cab. She wanted to go to the airport with me, but I have been caught once before getting into a cab with an audience member, I don't do that now, I'm a fast learner.

When I came down to the lobby, she didn't mess around. She said, " I have someone who you must see and it's urgent, when can you visit Melbourne?" I told her that my schedule didn't bring me there for another two months. "No, you have to see this person now, today or tomorrow at the latest", she said. By now the cab had pulled up and I was indicating to her that I needed to go. As I walked towards the cab she suddenly caught hold of my arm, leaned over and whispered the name of who it was that she needed me to see. Up until that lady grabbed my arm I had always prided myself on being able to keep cool in any situation and take everything in my stride. She obviously learned a lot from me that day about breaking behaviour patterns and replacing them with new behaviours. When she saw the look on my face she added that this person was in the hotel and wanted to see me now.

I was finding it very difficult to believe what was being said to me. At first I dismissed it as a joke, that was until she said, "Please don't worry about getting back to Sydney tonight, when you are finished, we will have a plane standing by for you". That was interesting because my office had arranged for me as always to take the last flight that night back to Sydney. Now I was intrigued to say the least. Needless to say I went and did some nice work with this now well known Statesman. When it came to doing some work with his team, he told me he had already changed them. This surprised me a little, until he told me that a friend of his who I had worked with previously told him that I said his team was a load of shit.

I mentioned that the reason I told his friend that his team was shit, was because they never added value. They were simply there for the ride. I was glad to hear that my team thing was getting around on the celebrity circuit, but I hope I don't meet any ex-team members in a dark alley, who got their marching orders because of me. Time and again when celebrities ask for help they do it in the most unusual way. Then when you arrive to help them some of them just want to treat you like part of their team.

Now, I'm all for building a team around you to assist, but one such celebrity wanted me permanently which as you can imagine didn't thrill the life out of me. When I think about what I witnessed that day with her team of people, I am surprised she is still alive let alone still on the scene. For some reason this happens, you meet a singer and she wants to become an actress. You meet an actress and she wants to become a singer. What is it with these people? Why can't they be happy pumping millions of dollars into their bank accounts doing what they do best?

The Day I Met a Superstar

One particular lady was devastated that she didn't get a certain job on television. As she put it, she was just completely shattered. "So what do you want me to do?" I asked her. She yelled, "You're the Master Of Change, do something". Charming I thought, I couldn't believe this diminutive little sweet looking angel on television could lose her temper so quickly. "Okay" I said, "Stand up and tell me how bad it really is". She told me that her life was over in TV and that none of the networks would touch her. I asked her how she knew all this and she told me her agent told her. "How did your Agent know, how can you be so sure? Actually why don't you just commit suicide and save the network, your Agent and everyone else the trouble", and with that I began to walk out of her hotel room.

This is my way of interrupting her pattern of behaviour and the choice of language that she would respond to most. Well, my little language pattern shift really worked, no one had ever spoken to her like that before. "Just where do you think your going?" she screamed. "To get a cab and go home", I said. "Oh no you don't", she said. "I hired you for an hour and we haven't even been going ten minutes yet". I turned towards her and laughed and said, "Hey honey I haven't been paid a cent yet, so I'll send you an invoice for ten minutes and we will call it even". I was still walking across the room to leave when she decided to try the water dispensing (crying) idea. I immediately looked at her and told her that when she was finished feeling sorry for herself she could either jump out of the window or give me a call.

As I opened the door she walked over, stopped crying and apologised. I accepted her apology because it was sincere and the exchange of words between us had worked to interrupt her pattern of behaviour. It wasn't that pleasant for her, but my motto is whatever works for the client, do it.

"The trouble with you celebrities", I said, "Is you get too big for your own lunch time. Three days ago I was in New York, no one knows you in New York, are you aware of that?" I asked. "Yes" she said, "I know that".

I told her that the first thing she had to stop doing was beating herself up every time she missed out on a job. The second thing was to look forward to missing out on them in the future. She looked puzzled. I said, "Remember how you felt a little time ago. Well, imagine the next time you get a no, wouldn't it feel great if you felt really happy and content that you gave it your very best. It also saves you putting yourself through this nonsense every time". I was hedging my bets here, I knew as she was listening and thinking that she could either say bullshit or carry on.

I asked her how many times she applied for jobs and she said all the time. She would apply for an acting job in TV, films or theatre, anywhere she thought would be an opportunity. I asked her if she got them all and she told me that she didn't. "So you're in a business where you know from the outset that having a no said to you, is in fact part of the business, is this correct"? I asked. "Yes", she said.

I was on a roll and wanted to finish quickly so she could sit and think a while before her team appeared again. "Do you play sport?" I asked her. "Yes golf", she said. "Great now you know that Jack Nicklaus has lost more tournaments than he has won then?" I said. She smiled and said, "Yes". I said, "You also know that Jack has won more majors than any other human alive".

"Yes", she said. "Do you think that Jack knows that he will lose more than he wins?" I asked. "Yes", she answered. "Great well there you have it. You know you will receive a no more than a yes, so now tell me how you want to feel about the next no?" I said. She said, "I want to feel as though I had a good go". "Great", I said, "Then that's all you need to do". I continued, "Oh by the way, about your team, can you tell me what each of them contributes to your success?"

She wasn't ready for that question, she also wasn't ready to have someone talk to her the way I did. She was used to having people say yes to her all the time. How dumb is that? She couldn't answer the question about her team by the way, but I did make some progress. She asked me to see her again and I agreed. The next time was about four months later and her team was half the size. She was looking much better than the last time I saw her. I asked her what had changed. She said that she had changed. She said she had made up her mind about what it was she really wanted and started to live it daily. I can remember one of these no name celebrities having a stand up brawl with me all because I wouldn't agree with what he was saying to me. If you ever become a celebrity, whatever that is, please don't lose yourself in a world of make believe.

Famous people are no different than you. They have the same problems, anxieties and fears as anyone. For most of these famous people their life revolves around who they are and what they do. The famous people I work with are no different in my mind than working with a homeless person off the street. They have a head and two arms and legs, most of them have red blood and a heart. Although with some celebrities I always like to take their pulse as I shake hands, just in case.

I imagine that any celebrities who read this right now will be thinking either wow I need to see this guy or stuff him who needs him anyway. For my part people are people. Your team of experts that you create for yourself is a team only when you need them. You don't have to pay for them twenty-four hours a day like famous people do, so you are lucky. Working with very famous people as opposed to just minor league celebrities is a world apart. The A-List really know what they want. They just get stuck sometimes, just like anyone. What you can learn from really successful people is how they remain successful, while others disappear. They know how to keep themselves fresh and topical, they can reinvent who they are easily. It's something I suggest to couples all the time. That's why I have people bring along a photo, you can now take a tip from the big stars, go and reinvent yourself, be happy with who you are.

No matter whom you meet in life and no matter what feelings and tricks your mind may start to play on you there is always a way of dealing with it. One actress I worked with last year demonstrated how good she was at forming beliefs. She told me that every time she went for an audition she was able to really become the character, something she told me was vital for all actors. She could read a script and as she acted out the character in her mind, she was able to form a belief that she took over the behaviour of the character she would play. I wasn't there to have a lesson in acting, she had asked me to help her because she wasn't getting many roles. In other words, she like the rest of these people in the industry lose out on getting the part often. Her audition figures were really bad though, she would get one part, but it would take her 30 auditions. She told me that she travelled overseas regularly for auditions, worked hard on forming her belief about the character and still didn't win many parts.

So I had her form a new belief. This new belief was that she would get the very next job she went for. She was good at forming a character belief, but found this new belief a little difficult at first, so I had her pretend the new belief was for a new character. The new character was in fact herself. By making the new belief as she had always done (for a character) it was easier for her. We really worked on having all the ingredients she needed to include in her new belief.

When she told me what her present belief was, it was little wonder that she had to go to so many auditions. She worked really well at creating a new belief for herself, and then all we needed to do was have her associate into that belief. That was easy, all I had her do was imagine that she was on stage. How easy was that for her? You see you only need to use what you are good at, and then add these wonderful techniques. I received a call from her some months later and she told me that she got the very next part she went for. Over the months she had got her average down to just one part won in only ten auditions. She said she was getting more parts offered to her without auditions, which was wonderful. The more she won parts, the stronger the belief grew, how's that for planning a great future?

Tips To Make You Feel Amazing

Model Success

Look what the successful people do. They have a clear understanding of what it is they want. The way to do this is to see it in your minds eye, feel it, smell it, touch it. Your senses are the key to making your future what you want it to be. So make sure you know exactly what it is you want.

Plan It

Have a plan that keeps you on course. Make sure your plan is flexible, so if it's not getting you what you want, you can easily change it.

Fire It Up

Every successful person I have ever worked with or met has been able to get fired up (excited) about what it is they desire. When you become passionate about your present and your future, your mind produces all the symptoms of that reality. So you are drawn towards it.

Believe It

Make a belief that your outcome is real enough and you will begin to form the belief that it actually will happen, and of course it will. Also reduce any beliefs that have stopped you from what it is you want to do. Reduce its impact and size and feel the belief shrink.

Good Or Bad

Whenever you look at a situation to attempt to decide which decision to make, list the good and the bad, then see if you can cross out as many bad ones as possible by saying to yourself, is this really that bad?

Take Some Action

People win by competing, if you are not competing in your life, how will you win? Take action, any action and once you keep taking more action you'll discover that being out of a once comfort zone is in fact enjoyable. You won't want to be safe ever again.

Major In The Big Stuff

Once you have propelled yourself into action you can then begin to prioritise the big stuff. Selecting what it is you need to concentrate on and leaving the minor stuff alone. The more you keep completing the big stuff, the quicker you reach your outcome.

Enjoy The Ride

Whenever you go for something, enjoy the journey, not the destination. You may want to earn five million dollars, but while you are getting it, why not stop and smell the roses. Take your time to balance things in your life and never give up precious people in your life for the wasted pursuit of money.

Naked In Front Of The Mirror

Start planning how you want to feel in twelve months and three years. Here is how to start now. Tonight go and undress and stand naked in front of a full length mirror and for sixty seconds only look at your face, nothing else. Now, I can almost hear your mind saying, what the?

Don't do this with children around, they will ask questions that you will never be able to answer. Don't do it with anyone around. This is your assignment for 60 seconds only. Also don't leave the curtains open, we don't want to hear about you on the local news networks. Just take a few minutes on your own, take all your clothes off and stand in front of a full-length mirror and only look at your face. Then do it again the morning after and continue to do this for three days and three nights, and then stop doing it.

Okay, so your mind might be wondering what on earth this is all about or what you will get out of doing this exercise? I want you to do this exercise as soon as you have finished the book. Look at your face. After all you take your face out with you every day. You take your face to work and all the time other people are going to look at it. I want you to promise yourself that you will do this exercise. You have got this far in the book, so you know that what we have done so far works, so when your mind doubts this, tell it to piss off. Just do it.

It might also be an idea to have a pen and paper with you when you do this wonderful exercise. Once you have finished the 60 second drill, I want you to immediately write down what you said to yourself.

Here's what I want you to do next on your assignment list. When you are in the company of strangers I want you to pull the funniest and biggest grin you possibly can and hold it while you look at someone for sixty seconds. So again, please pick your people carefully. Find a person and make a really big funny grinning smile and hold it for sixty seconds.

Like the assignment before, your conscious mind will be inserting dumb questions for you. Don't let your conscious mind take over, this is the exercise, just go out and do it.

Now the last assignment for you is this one. It's one that I seem to get the most feedback on and I can't think why. Here's what to do. Next time you are again in the company of strangers, even some acquaintances, I want you to have a normal conversation with them and as you do, I want you to suddenly and carefully lie down on the floor on your back and keep talking to them, just like nothing has happened at all. Stay on the floor for about two minutes chatting away as normal and then get back on your feet and continue the conversation just as normal, as if nothing had happened. Now to do this assignment correctly you must keep talking as you go down on your back. Don't suddenly stop talking and then drop to the floor.

Warning, don't do this outside in the rain, you'll get wet. Don't do it with children, because they will just do what you did and then both of you will be lying on your back. Now, as you can understand your conscious mind might be saying things to you like, Patrick you're kidding me or don't do it. Simply take control and do the exercise.

Another fun exercise to do is go into a photo booth (they are normally in shopping centres) and take some stupid pictures, like really pull silly faces and have a really silly time. Then as you are introduced to new people, open your wallet or purse and show them your photos and tell them that this is as serious as you can be.

One of the easiest ways for you to program an outcome of feeling really good all the time is to reduce your limiting belief about being serious. I have never met anyone who said to me they were suffering from depression, and then burst out laughing. Have you heard the phrase, *One day I'll look back on this and laugh*? Why wait. Laugh now! There is absolutely no reason why you should even want to be serious anymore in your life. It doesn't do you any good, so work on being stupid, silly, and outrageous or any other feeling that fits you.

Now your conscious mind may want to argue with this but by now you have the idea, don't judge it until you do it first. Just go out and be silly and really mean it. I have been looked at plenty of times for some of my more outrageous behaviour but it made me feel wonderful. The funny thing is the people doing the observing took on the state of being serious when they did their observation. Think about how wild that is. It's like being on a freeway and while your driving some other driver does something you think isn't right, so you go into your serious state. Now you can do what I do when that happens, laugh and enjoy it.

Conclusion

I hope you have enjoyed reading my book and gained many ideas along the way. My objective in writing this book was to share with you how people, ordinary people, no matter what colour, creed or age live amazing lives. What I have witnessed along my own personal journey has been remarkable. Like the people that have walked in my office ready to end their life only to leave motivated to live their dream.

Parents that lost their way who suddenly have no fear anymore and they bring their family together again. Couples that have competed with each other in their marriage for years have learned they can live happily together. Celebrities who have gone from the brink of self-disaster to suddenly re-launching their careers and lives again.

Grandmother's who have found a mission in their life and turned sorrow into safety. The list is far too long to fit into this text. What I wanted to do was inspire you to be inspired from within. No one else can give you the life you always wanted, only you. I hope now you realise it isn't scary or difficult it's a matter of you making a decision, that's all you need to do, *decide.*

I am certain that as you read through this book time and time again and discuss it with friends and loved ones, that the nuggets of gold hidden in these pages will come to light your journey for you. I am also willing to bet you that when you make that decision to live an amazing life that the world will make an about face and turn towards you. The world on hearing and reading your written goals will then work with you. You are a magnet. Whatever you put your mind to will arrive in your life, so remember to *want* good things, not think about all the things you don't want. I urge you to do the Law Of Attraction exercise at least three times a year so it gives you clarity and direction.

Everyone you look at and admire today has gone through what you, I and others go through, however that person you admire looked inside their soul and discovered what was most important to them and spent their life doing what they love and loving what they do. I again urge you to follow your dream and not let uncertainty or other people stop you.

Please remember this very important point. Your body provides emotions and feeling that provide you with feedback. It is this very feedback that you need to understand. Make sure you don't trick your mind, otherwise your feedback will be off. Your body is the real key to living an amazing life, listen to it, refine it, make sure its real and then enjoy feeling amazing.

If your body begins to feel uneasy or anxious do my 60 Second Challenge and make sure you clear your body first. You will discover that when you use this powerful technique as often as I do it becomes part of the way you make decisions. Clear your body so it feels good and then move into a powerful, excited state and then make a decision.

When you are asked at the end of your life, did you do everything you wanted to do in your life, you want to be able to say, oh yes I did, I truly did.

Thank you for reading my book. May you live a truly amazing life.

Best Wishes …

Patrick McNally PhD

Patrick McNally PhD

Patrick conducts workshops and lectures worldwide.
Many of these lectures are created by organisations that want to share a message with their customers and audiences. Patrick is often hired to deliver their message. Should your company need to deliver a message that will impact your audiences positively then contact Patrick at his website.

He also trains staff and consults to small, medium and large business enterprises. Today more than ever business needs to invest in its people. To have a motivated team living your company dream is a goal that can be achieved. If your company and staff need to go that extra step and truly excel then contact Patrick at his website.

He helps couples resolve issues and live happily. There isn't a person on the planet that doesn't want to have a long loving relationship. Today that goal appears to be getting more and more difficult. Patrick's proven strategies for a lasting relationship shows couples the true *how to* of relationships.

Addictions are normally very difficult to break however Patrick has a proven method that involves everyone connected with the sufferer. If you truly want help in this area for you or someone in your life contact Patrick through his website.

To purchase any of his products or for further information please visit his personal website at: www.patrick-mcnally.com

Also Books By Patrick McNally PhD

How To Have An Amazing Mind E-Book
A book that gives you all the powerful techniques to change your life

How To Have Amazing Relationships
The ultimate relationship book filled with exercises and tips.

Audio Programs

Learn To Relax
Learn to relax, sleep deeper and feel calm all the time.

www.patrick-mcnally.com

Acknowledgements

It takes teamwork to make a book come to life and the team assembled for this book has been extraordinary. I'd like to begin by thanking Mark Knopfler for writing "Local Hero Wild Theme" which was in my ears playing along through the entire time I was writing this. I will forever be indebted to his magnificent guitar playing and musical arrangements. He is a man who lives an amazing life.

To the clients that have been kind enough to allow me to help them over the years, I thank each and every one of you. By working with you it has enabled me to refine my skills and develop even more profound techniques that help others. So even in your darkest moments that you shared with me, not only did we turn your life into an amazing one, your truth and courage ensured that you helped others along the way. I am eternally grateful to you.

My thanks also go to Ellen, Donna, Tracy and Mary for their help in reading my early drafts. Your opinions and suggestions were pure nuggets of gold, thank you.

To my loving and patient wife Irene, thank you again for all your support and the rest of the family my thanks to you for putting up with everything that goes with having a writer in the family. You are all amazing thank you.

When we are born, we begin to grow into young people and then into adults. As we grow a few things begin to change along the way. The most important change begins early as an infant.

You see, when you were laying in your dirty nappy screaming the house down, you didn't care about anyone else. You didn't lay on the floor totally naked at 12 months old and scream out, "Mummy for God's sake woman put some clothes on me, I'm embarrassed".

No you couldn't because you couldn't speak, you didn't have a conscious mind, that's the voice inside your head that today as an adult can keep you awake at night. Do you know the one I mean?

My mother once told me this old tale. She said, "My son there are only two things in life you need worry about. First ask yourself are you well or sick. If you are well, you have nothing to worry about.

If you are sick you only have two things that can happen, you will either live of die. If you live you have nothing to worry about. So if you die you only have two things that can happen.

You will either go to heaven or hell. If you go to heaven nothing will happen. If you go to hell you will be so busy catching up with all your friends you won't have time to worry".

Mary (Maisie) McNally

www.ingramcontent.com/pod-product-compliance
Lightning Source LLC
Chambersburg PA
CBHW060754050426
42449CB00008B/1405